The Sounds of Worship

(The Cult of Sound)

David H. Dirks

A practical handbook for ministers, worship leaders, musicians, and technical crews on the challenges in bringing our gifts and talents and the technology we use into submission to authentic worship

ISBN: 9798668291649
Independently published

Cover design by: Art Painter

Printed in the United States of America

Endorsements

What would worship in our churches be like if technical staff, musicians, and pastors worked together in *harmony* for one purpose: to bring authentic *glory to God*? As an insider who has served in this arena for decades, Dirks understands the dishonoring dissonance that often occurs instead. With a lively and provocative writing style, he clearly lays out technical and human challenges and offers abundantly helpful suggestions. *The Sounds of Worship* is a significant gift to the church.

Dennis H. Dirks, Ph.D., Professor Emeritus I Dean, Talbot School of Theology (retired), Dean of Academic Administration, Biola University (retired)

There's a simple question church leadership and worship teams almost never address, that of the nature of authentic worship in an age of technology. With Biblical insight and technical guidance David Dirks ushers readers into a conversation that can transform church life. Both practical and provocative, Sounds of Worship will help congregations more clearly hear what God has to say.

Dan Barnett, book columnist, Chico Enterprise-Record

David Dirks' new book *The Sounds of Worship* is a must read for today's musicians and sound techs that lead and produce the music for our Sunday worship services. In a systematic style David reminds us that we do not worship the "sound of our voice, an instrument played, the mixed sound, or the technology that enhances sound." We worship the Creator of sound!

Worship leaders, church musicians, and sound techs must continually be reminded of this truth if our worship is to be God honoring and authentic.

A. Merril Smoak, Jr., D.W.S., Adjunct Professor, Gateway Seminary, San Francisco Campus, Dean, Jubilee College of Music, Olivet University

The sound tech is as much a part of the worship band as any musician on stage. Playing the sound board as their instrument, they contribute to the experience and atmosphere of worship as much as any vocalist. David's book is a rare culmination of technical excellence and spirit-lead creative. It is my go-to textbook on the subject of sound, leadership and engineering in worship.

Brad Sousa, Chief Technology Officer, AVI Systems, Inc.

In an age of rapidly changing technological advances, David Dirks provides us an important understanding of how acoustics and audiovisual equipment can either enhance or detract from the church corporate worship experience. Too often, as pastors, worship leaders and sound technicians, we had believed that if there was some kind of sound amplification, everything was okay. David shared valuable information concerning the importance of authentic, Biblically based worship. Then David revealed how to enhance our worship by upgrading the acoustics in a facility, as well as adding some of the technological advances available to churches to enhance the worship experience for those in attendance. I highly suggest that every pastor, worship leader or church audiovisual technician obtain and read a copy of his book and keep it as a resource in their library. David's expertise has certainly enhanced the worship experience in our church. It is also a good reminder that anything we do for God should be accomplished with excellence, not just so it is good enough. God deserves the very best!

Andy Cochran, Senior Pastor, Brentwood Bible Fellowship, Brentwood, CA

If you serve in any part of the music ministry—and you want your craft to be in submission to the Lord Jesus—this book is for you. *The Sounds of Worship* confronts us with the brutal ramifications of music, technology, and self-aggrandizement. It is a call to place ourselves under the authority of Jesus as we worship in Sprit and truth.

Dr. Nathan Morales, Pastor at Hilltop Church & author at *gospelgeeks.net*

This book (my first) is fondly dedicated to my wife Karen, whose brightly shining light is the light of Christ.

Contents

Thesis

The Sounds of Worship are a God-pleasing aroma when we worship Him authentically in spirit and in truth. He is intensely jealous for us and seeks our worship. At times, though, we allow the focus of our worship to move from Him, the Creator of all things, to the worship of created things. When we exalt our talents and abilities and elevate our technology as the source of the power in worship, we turn worship on its head. We practice "the cult of sound." God's command is to bring all created things into submission to the authority He has given us to rule the earth. We worship Him and Him alone.

Introduction

Several years ago, I was setting up for a concert with a well-known and respected gospel singer. The singer walked into the auditorium early in the afternoon of the concert, before anyone else, for a sound check. As he entered, he asked in his trademark baritone tones, "Are you sound?"

What followed was an engaging moment as we discussed the meaning of the question. This book addresses the idea directly and asks the questions: Are you sound? Do you have a theology of sound? Are the sounds that you make, whether as a musician or an engineer, consistent with sounds that honor and glorify Christ? Or are you finding yourself seduced into worshiping the sounds you make or the sounds you manage? Fundamentally, sounds of worship should be a biblically-based theology and not just the mechanics of good sound.

All too often, we engage only in discussing the technical aspects and the techniques of making sound. In a world where technology is stuffed into every corner of our lives, it is almost impossible to function without the distractions of a plethora of digital devices— smartphones (and emerging direct eye retina display), smart TVs (smart enough to follow your every move), watches, pads, autonomous and self-driving cars, and Artificial Intelligence (AI) aware sound systems. Yet, we are called as disciples of Christ to worship the Creator, not the technology, not the creation.

As a pastor, worship leader, sound engineer/tech or musician, are the sounds you produce for worship theologically sound?

Typical Sunday Service

It's Sunday morning. Eight a.m. Services start in one hour, and only three of the six band members are present. The setup time is 7 a.m., but few rarely make it on time. The previous week's rehearsal had been canceled due to conflicting schedules, and now the bandleader is anxious. The band has not played the intro song in months. It has a tricky start, and the leader knows the band is not ready to play it.

The Front of House[1] (FOH), the person who mixes the sound for the congregation, is on his cell phone and not paying attention to the completion of the setup on stage. Nothing is ready. The pastor walks into the sanctuary, stops, looks at the stage, and asks, "Where is everyone?" The bandleader shrugs his shoulders. The pastor shakes his head with a frown and takes a few steps. He stops for a moment and motions to the FOH. "I've got a video for the announcements. When do you want it?" The FOH does not acknowledge the pastor but keeps talking on the phone. "Not sure whether the sound is any good on the video," the pastor says in elevated tones and adds, "Can you test it?" But the FOH doesn't hear.

A loud thump is heard in the room, and everyone jumps. The sound system has just been turned on. One of the vocalists starts tapping hard on a microphone. "Is this thing on? I can't hear anything!" The lead guitarist is now on stage and slams his gear into motion. Before long, he is playing licks without paying attention to anyone or anything. "Am I loud enough out there?" he yells to the FOH. Without adjusting anything, the FOH shakes his head yes and groans under his breath. The bandleader turns to one of the singers and says with dripping sarcasm, "It's Sunday morning!"

Is this story an exaggeration? I don't think so. I have seen this scene time and time again in many different forms. If you can identify with any portion of the story, this book is for you. It is not untypical for many members of the band and the sound team to be unprepared for Sunday morning. The lack of preparation and passion for worship has led some to question whether our modern, expensive sound systems are necessary in the first place.

The Necessity of Sound

While sound is necessary for worship (e.g., being able to hear the words spoken or sung), a sound system and the support infrastructure and staff are not. Sophisticated sound reinforcement and support staff are a modern phenomenon. The question then arises, how was the good news of the Bible communicated for nearly 2000 years without a sound system? Jesus spoke to thousands without artificial sound reinforcement. Spurgeon preached to thousands without a single piece of technology, and, amazingly, the spoken word was heard and received. In contrast, today's church has made sound (and other technology) central to what happens when we gather as the body of Christ to worship. A great deal of energy and money is applied to sound structures without much concern for whether the energy and monetary investment are truly God-honoring. We seem not to be able to function without it.

We have transformed our worship into a cult[2] that worships our efforts and the product of our efforts. The cult centers on the sounds we make rather than worship of the Creator. When we pour so many resources (time, effort, money) into our worship services, we invoke the impression that the hour (or whatever amount of time) we spend singing is the only time we are truly worshiping. It is rather telling that we spend so much time on the topic of a corporate worship service rather than the whole of our lives.

Central to the premise of this book is that Christian worship is far more than what happens during a worship service on Sunday morning (or any other time of the week). Within the Christian faith exists a far grander perspective on worship. Worship is not just a one-hour event. Yet the problems and challenges we see in the worship services are reflective of the greater issues with worship in our own lives.

We have learned how to compartmentalize all aspects of life. Our work life, our church life, our home life, our this-is-for-me part of life divisions can be very isolated with boundaries that do not cross. However, Christ calls us to a different type of relationship, a different view of ourselves and the world. He calls us to see the totality of all things wrapped up in Christ and Christ alone.

The Book Is Not This

This book is not intended to be the authority on sound for worship, nor is it intended to explain the intricate mechanics and technology needed to build a quality sound reinforcement system. The important mechanics (according to this author) are explained here but not in detail. A plethora of books on the market covers both worship and the mechanics of sound design and operations. Those resources are referenced in the bibliography. Neither is this book intended for those involved with large venue sound or the recording artist.

It's This

According to Barna,[3] thirty-six percent of those who attend church regularly attend a church with 101 to 499 in attendance. Forty-six percent attend a church with less than 100 persons. I believe these average sized churches are the ones that can benefit from some of the insights and professional experience presented in this book.

The average church may not have access to professionally trained musicians and crews. Those churches, for lack of a better example, may end up following the trends of the bigger church (attempting to emulate what appears to be successful) or fall back to secular trends. Whether the desire is to look more professional or to be culturally relevant, the church worship services migrated a long time ago from simple acoustic instruments to greater and greater dependence on technology. Whatever the reason for increasing the dependency on technology, it is crucial that those in leadership not lose sight of the limitations of technology. More importantly, leadership must understand the impact technology imposes on worship, for good and for bad.

Central to the theme of this book is a definition of authentic worship. Congregational worship and our attitudes regarding our abilities, sounds, and the talent we bring to worship are measured against that definition. Much of the lack of authentic worship in today's worship services stems from a lack of proper preparation by all involved—not just the pastors or leaders. In this book, I address that issue directly.

An additional premise of this book is that we fail to worship authentically when we depend on technology to draw in and entertain the congregation. The work of worship leaders is to point to Christ and to build an atmosphere to not inhibit the work of the Holy Spirit nor distract the worshiper's attention from God and God alone. I also will explore an issue that is lacking in awareness and discussion. I ask a simple question: Can worship leaders, singers, musicians, and members of the technical crew enter into worship while performing their duties? I believe the answer to this question reveals our fundamental attitudes about worship.

Why I Wrote This Book

The impetus for writing this book grew out of my experiences that started in the early 1970s. When I graduated from college, I started a sound recording studio and venue sound services company. The school of hard knocks taught me much about quality sound. I was soon asked and agreed to volunteer to set up and run sound for the church I attended. A pivotal experience was in the late 70s when I met Dr. Merril A. Smoak Jr. Merril was called as Music Minister for Trinity Baptist Church in Livermore, California. In those days, the Music Minister was expected to lead all music and run the sound system at the same time. The mixing console sat on stage, right next to where Merril sat.

Merril and I met at a church event before his first Sunday as Music Minister, and we struck up an immediate friendship and working relationship around worship and the requirements of sound for worship. The timing of our meeting was significant. Within a couple of years, Trinity built a new building with a 500-seat auditorium.

The first Sunday in the new building taught us volumes about acoustics and sound and how both directly impact the service. Though the congregation was 500 persons strong, Merril found it impossible to hear the congregation singing. The senior pastor, Dr. James Morton, was frustrated with the echo/slap-back from the back wall that gave his voice the sound of a large stadium. Through the building program and the years following, we cut our teeth on the functional application of sound, acoustics, physics, and technology in worship.

Almost forty years later, Merril and I are still working, discussing, and honing our skills and understanding, and passing the knowledge to students in the Master of Divinity program at Gateway seminary.

In writing this book, I have the conviction that like John the Baptist's proclamation in John 3:30, "He must increase, but I must decrease," sound for worship must be much more and at the same time much, much less. More attention needs to be applied to the details and the teamwork that brings the music and the spoken word to the congregation.

At the same time, those of us involved should strive for a less noticeable presence. Sound should not say, "Here I am." Sound or technology is not the object of our worship. Neither are we. Rather, the mechanics of sound and the technology are mere servants to the end goal. Sound should seamlessly reinforce the worship time, unnoticeable, receiving no glory. All glory should go to God. This book is an attempt to draw together the biblically based principles to help the reader achieve a heartfelt quality sound that is not disruptive, distracting, nor desiring of attention.

I am mindful of the admonition of the call to worship in Romans 12 as a call to sacrifice ourselves and our desires in order to worship. We are called to be "transformed by the renewing of our minds." As I write this manuscript, the evangelical world recently celebrated the 500th anniversary of Martin Luther's Reformation. Luther was transformed by his profound understanding of the imputed righteousness of Christ that led to the profound reformation of the Christian church in thought and practice.

As Luther was renewed by the Word, we are called to be a people transformed by the Word that in turn leads to a reformation of practice.[4] The traditions of the world—particularly the reliance and dependence on technology as the place where we turn first to solve problems—must be rejected. Our faithfulness to the Word of God and its transforming, reforming, and renewing power is where we must live.

I find myself convicted and conflicted at times. The very thing I believe I desire to achieve in my work may be missing biblical principles. I am struck by the biblical admonishment to do all things in love. It absolutely does not matter how skilled, talented, or gifted I am, if I do not love, according to 1 Corinthians 13, I am just moving console sliders, strumming guitar strings, and pushing buttons.

My prayer and desire are that whether you are pastor, minister, musician, technician, or engineer, you will find this book helpful in the daily decisions you make regarding worship and the sounds we create for worship. I also desire that the topics will spark discussions within church leadership. Ask the question: Are the sounds you produce or manage for worship a cult of sound or authentic worship.

PART I

The Cult of Sound

You Are What You Worship

Chapter 1

Wars and Rumors of Wars

"If you turn back your foot from the Sabbath, from doing your pleasure on my holy day, and call the Sabbath a delight and the holy day of the Lord honorable; if you honor it, not going your own ways, or seeking your own pleasure, or talking idly; then you shall take delight in the Lord, and I will make you ride on the heights of the earth" (Isaiah 58:13-14).

Several years ago, after joining a new church, I was approached to provide leadership for the sound and media team. The church was having problems with a poor sound system and a lackluster mix on Sunday morning. Before the work to make improvements ever began, I boldly spouted off, "I hate working with musicians." To which the bandleader responded, "I hate sound guys, always have."

Though there was a bit of tongue in cheek in those proclamations, they do not sound edifying. Over time I came to understand the underpinning philosophy both of us possessed and often expressed. The statements revealed a gritty honesty and experience-hammered truthfulness regarding music in the modern evangelical church. Underneath the words percolated a passion (sometimes in frustration) for the kind of worship that is correct, authentic, and honors God, not us. The bandleader and I had worked in both church and professional venues, as recording/sound engineer and drummer/singer. Both of us were wearied of the ubiquitous and tired attitudes of grandiose self-importance.

That interchange and the conversations in the ten years that followed were, as they say in show business, the start of a wonderful relationship. The two of us have worked intentionally to apply the principles laid out in this book and develop authentic worship patterns, music, and relationships. We buried our dislikes and prejudices and moved forward.

We take every opportunity to encourage, train, and understand each other. The relationship is loving, respectful, and complementary. And even though some believe the worship bandleader should be the boss, both of us lead and make decisions that are best for our areas of expertise in cooperation with each other and the other members of the team. We see the worship team as everyone involved, not just musicians. The attitude that everyone is serving together is an absolute key to success.

The work is not without its detractions and failures. All too often, we fall flat—musically, technically, and relationally. Yet we are quick to get up again and remind each other that this is about Him, not us, about the congregation worshiping, not our lack of talent or gross mistakes. Sanctification[1] is an ongoing process; it is a journey, not an earthly destination. The work of sanctification takes time and intentional energy. At times it is unseen and unnoticed by others yet God-honoring—a glorious work. In contrast, some have thwarted the sanctification process and never get past, "I hate…"

Hate's Lifestyle

The "hate" may be for the style of music, or the way it's presented, or the personalities involved. Dislike and hatred are not uncommon between musicians and FOH, and sometimes between pastors, staff, and lay ministers. Though we may not admit it, hate perpetuates because of our selfish view of our gifts, talents, and vision.

In his book, True Worship—Seeking What Matters to God, Bob Kauflin states that worship has hit the big time. There is "an ever-increasing number of books, magazines, websites, and blogs devoted exclusively to the topic of worship, or at least worship music. *Worship has become a thing, if not the thing*. It's a movement, a phenomenon, and in many places, an industry [emphasis added]."

Kauflin goes on to list the "undeniable benefits" of an increased focus on worship, including an outpouring of new songs and a revitalization of congregational singing. He also says, "But it hasn't all been good. Heated arguments about worship music styles have divided or destroyed congregations. *Performance is often valued over participation, and technology over truth.* Many songs have been written by musicians who don't know their Bibles very well, resulting in songs that lack gospel and theological clarity. Worst of all, worship has been reduced almost universally to what happens when we sing [emphasis added]." [2]

Anything that distracts, whether it be dislike or hatred of style or persons involved, anything that causes us not to look to Christ and Christ alone as we worship is sin. How can we claim or ask for the Lord's blessings in our services if we dishonor His name through selfish bickering and infighting? How can we call on others to imitate those of us visible in worship, as Paul does,[3] if our worship is for ourselves, our music, our style, our tech, or our desires? When Christ's disciples wanted to be granted positions of power over the kingdom to come, Jesus brought crystal clarity to the subject when He said, "For even the Son of Man came not to be served but to serve, and to give his life as a ransom for many." [4]

Losing sight of our place in the kingdom is quite easy to do. The world has promoted measures for success that involve power, money, authority, and fame. Read any self-help book or look at any professional blog or social media. Success in this world is about me and my accomplishments.

In stark contrast, the kingdom of God is not about me. It is only about Him. As we lead and provide the critical support functions for worship, I believe we should be asking the question: What is the biblical imperative that guides worship, rather than insisting on what we want, have to have, or desire?

Question: When mixing the sound, playing an instrument, singing lead or backup, running the slides, or being the person who is responsible for all that takes place, whom or what do you worship?

Consuming Worship

As musicians and ministers have placed an increasing emphasis on worship as an experience, the rise in the use of technology associated with worship has exploded. To many, the use of tech and theatrical techniques is obligatory. An overarching principle has emerged that we are turning people away and not reaching the intended demographics if we do not look, act, dress, and sound culturally friendly. Instead of being consumed by the all-consuming fire of the Holy Spirit, too often we are consuming the event as an enjoyable diversion or secular concert.

How many times have we heard the New Age phrase, "If you build it, they will come"? Rod Dreher characterizes the problem as one of consumerism. "American Christians have a bad habit of treating church like a consumer experience. If the congregation doesn't meet our felt needs, we are quick to find another one that we believe will."[5] American consumers have turned the church, the body of Christ, into a consumer experience where it is not uncommon to rate a church and the church experience with so many stars on Yelp. Applying the worldly perspective and consumer experience to worship makes it easy to lose sight of the reasons why we gather corporately.

The drift (some may call it a shift) toward consumerisms has been subtle and laced with pragmatic good intentions. Some have traced the change back to the adoption of a tent meeting revival format. In the last forty years, the simple addition of coffee and snacks, while making us look friendlier and more social, can cause upheaval in what otherwise should be times of reverential, Christ-centric, corporate worship.

The constant flow up and down of those seeking nourishment during the service causes the congregation to move from a meaningful, serious, honoring time to a casual time of fellowship. Those who are serious about worship can be distracted and disgruntled by the constant interruptions. It also causes a mess of empty coffee cups, banana peels, and half-eaten cookies left on the floor or the seat of a consumer attendee.

Couple those behaviors with music that follows a worldly pattern, and congregants not serious about authentic worship may view the service as just another time of fellowship with friends, a more casual time than a serious one. These types of meetings often result in people carrying on sidebar conversations and checking Facebook, email, and chat.

Let me be clear. I am humbled to tears when I study God's requirements for worship. I realize deep inside that I am flawed and often do not take God's commands seriously. I can be much too casual in my approach. I have too often simply showed up without the proper preparation for God's holy event. As such, my intent is not to be hypercritical as much as I am asking questions and seeking dialog.

Nothing is wrong with coffee, snacks, and enjoyment of the fellowship time together. I often bring a cup of coffee to church if I am teaching a class or managing the sound. But I ask the question, when do the externals become a dangerous distraction to the time of worship? Do the externals enhance or distract from the authentic worship of God?

The deceptive emphasis on the worshiper as a consumer may have contributed to what some refer to as "worship wars." If you have been in the church for any period, you have seen the challenges presented as certain age groups or interest groups feel their self-interests and style trump all others.

The older generation wants hymns and feels betrayed if the traditional hymns are not sung on Sunday morning. Middle-aged congregants want more up-tempo music and want to sing songs they sing and hear every day on Christian radio, while the young may want a more formal environment that does not mimic what is seen in the world. The overarching philosophy seems to be based mistakenly on Paul's admonition: "I have become all things to all people, that by all means I might save some."[6]

Paul modified his behavior so as not to offend or put off the very people he was trying to reach for the gospel. Paul never compromised the faith or the gospel. Instead, he adjusted for his circumstances. The overarching purpose of changing behavior was not to draw attention to himself or his style. Instead, more than perhaps anyone else at the time, Paul understood the nexus of our faith is not rooted in the externals or superficial. When with Jews, he ate kosher. When with Gentiles, he ate all foods offered to him.

A while back, I joined with others from our church to participate in a mission trip to South Korea. For most of those traveling, this was their first time visiting a foreign country. During the extensive training process, we were given particular instructions by the leaders of the mission trip regarding how we should act while visiting and ministering, which included specific dos and don'ts.

Some of the pastors on the trip were slated to visit dignitaries and business leaders. They were advised to be careful not to offend their hosts with stubborn American ways. When visiting a business leader or dignitary, the host might offer the pastor/missionary an alcoholic beverage to celebrate their meeting. Pastors were told not to refuse the drink as it would offend the host and perhaps close the door to effective witnessing. Many pastors had trouble with the instructions. It became a mixed response as to whether to accept the drink or not.

My point is not about drinking alcohol when offered or to be critical of pastors who struggled in the situation. Rather, it is to emphasize that Paul's approach in "becoming all things to all people" was in regards to evangelizing and witnessing—not about worship. Worship is about us conforming to God's pattern for authentic worship and not about the accommodation of individual styles and preferences.[7] "All things to all people" must be our context as we seek to engage all peoples of all cultures. It is not our attitude when we enter into a unique and specially dedicated time of corporate worship.

Six Generations[8] Share in Worship

Some people have gone so far as to describe the worship wars as "worship disrupters." In a modern sense, disrupters can be viewed as anything oblique to the conventional wisdom that overturns the previous ways of thinking. Generally, disruption is embraced to make progress, no matter how painful the process.

A column in Sound and Communications magazine[9] discussed disrupters and categorizes each based on whether they are "Intentionalists," who build services around Broadway type plays or concerts; "Modernists," who use Intentionalists' techniques but are more conservative; and "Traditionalists," who still sing hymns and maybe some praise songs with minimal technology. The column concludes that disruptors, changing the style of worship to accommodate age-related preferences, are good for change.

For the first time in history, we have as many as six generations[10] attending services. Each age group comes with highly individualized concepts and expectations on what constitutes worship. The first group is the GI Generation, born 1901-1926. The next group is the Mature/Traditionalists/Silent Generation, born 1927-1945, followed by the Baby Boomers, born 1946-1964. The Boomers have two distinct subsets: the save-the-world revolutionaries of the 60s/70s and the career climbers—the Yuppies and DINKS (double income no kids)—of the 70s/80s.

The next group is Generation X, born 1965-1980. Generation Y, generally called Millennials, were born 1981-2000. Finally, Generation Z/Boomlets were born after 2001. The defining moment for Gen Z is September 11, 2001.

In an effort to please, worship styles have bent so drastically that leaders are burning out from attempting to provide different experiences for different age groups. Some of these churches have three distinct worship services designed for segmented age groups and preferences. Workers have reported they are experiencing burnout and are returning to one style.

While mainstream churches choose to propel themselves down the post-Christian, post-modern cultural tracks with services designed to attract and appeal to the senses, some churches have unplugged. A movement to abandon amplified sound and return to the basics of acoustic instruments and un-amplified vocals and seek a calmer, more reverential style is happening in some churches.[11]

While much research has been accumulated on the various age groups and how each relates to and impact society, the work of the kingdom of God is not about tailoring or designing congregational worship for one group or another. All are members of one body. All worship the same and only God as one—together. The differences and affinities of each age group demonstrate the creative nature of God and should never become divisive.

When we divide by generation or preference, we divide the body of Christ arbitrarily. No such divisions are supported in Scripture. The Apostle Paul says,

> *Do you not know that you [the church, the body of Christ] are God's temple and that God's Spirit dwells in you? If anyone destroys God's temple, God will destroy him. For God's temple is holy, and you are that temple.* 1 Corinthians 3:16-17

To destroy God's temple is to cause disorder, dissension, or dysfunction. Paul is saying if you disrupt the body of Christ, God's temple, God will bring disorder upon you.

When we hold up the concept of disruption to worship and compare it with biblical standards, disrupting worship should be an anathema (detested or loathed) rather than a theme. As we will discuss later, worship is continuous fellowship with the Creator. Entering a humble and reverential place of fellowship with Christ is not dependent on a style or type of music, the color of the room, or the state of the lighting or my personal preferences for such. When Jesus' disciples asked Him how to pray, Jesus said,

> *And when you pray, you must not be like the hypocrites. For they love to stand and pray in the synagogues and at the street corners, that they may be seen by others. Truly, I say to you, they have received their reward. But when you pray, go into your room and shut the door and pray to your Father who is in secret. And your Father who sees in secret will reward you. And when you pray, do not heap up empty phrases as the Gentiles do, for they think that they will be heard for their many words. Do not be like them, for your Father knows what you need before you ask him.* (Matthew 6:5-8)

Jesus is noticeably clear about our prayer life. Those who pray in public to be seen by others have received their reward for their prayers. In other words, those who like to show off and exhibit their talents so others will notice them may receive public recognition, but that will be all they receive. The reward is not from our Father in heaven.

When we worship, we begin first in our personal worship closet and then bring that worship with us when we gather corporately. We bring the attitude of heartfelt worship as a member of the large congregation in worship. Dr. Harold Best uses the term "overheard worship."[12] As we are worshiping, we are overhearing and joining in the worship of those around us. If we are at war with each other, we are not about the holy work of worship.

Wars Without and Within

Worship wars are not new. Church building and style wars have been ever-present in my lifetime. When I was growing up, I experienced the battles and hurt feelings over where the piano should be placed. An often-repeated adage was, "Pie-ano on the right and organ on the left." In those days, churches split over which side of the church those two instruments were placed. When the traditional hymns were replaced with praise music and the addition of drums and electric guitars, some felt that the church had become apostate.

Wars and hurt feelings may develop over the color of the walls, or in the case of our church, the wallpaper. When we were completing a new church building in Livermore, California, in the late 70's, a few women of the church spent countless hours wall- papering the sanctuary. The finished product was nothing less than spectacular, and the women were proud of it.

When we discovered that the sanctuary acoustics were a disaster, a professional acoustician was hired to make the room measurements and recommend a solution. The solution, in part, was to cover the beautifully papered walls with thick acoustical treatment. Overnight, the hard work of those dedicated women disappeared, and the hurt feelings were evident. Those of us involved in the sound ministry were blamed for ruining the sanctuary and the hard work of those women.

Feelings and emotions can easily become wrapped and entangled in what we deem important. Jesus said, "For where your treasure is, there will your heart be also."[13] If the emphasis is on me (my work, my will, my way), then problems will result, and some of the problems can lead to deep divisions. Attitudes and wars do considerable damage to the kingdom of God.

In one of the churches I attended, one of the older members of the congregation demonstrated her personal preference regarding music by not attending the first half of the morning worship service. She visibly protested the removal of hymns and hymnals from the service by the new pastor. Each Sunday she sat in the car until the singing was complete, then entered the service during the offertory and in time for the sermon. She was faithful to this pattern every Sunday. Her husband, on the other hand, a founder of the church and longtime deacon, participated in singing the new songs without his wife. When asked about the changes, he said, "I don't agree with them, but I am not going to stand in the way of the Lord's progress."

Unfortunately, the deacon's wise perspective is not the norm. We typically don't think our attitudes are a hindrance to the work of the Holy Spirit! The deacon taught a great lesson simply by not standing in the way or insisting on his way. He could have battled against the changes and against the new pastor who had removed the hymns and hymnals. He could have let others know how displeased he was and break the unity of the Spirit. But he did not. He bit his tongue for the sake of unity and for the sake of the gospel.

When is change indeed required, and when is it the Lord's progress, and not our own? How can we know that the changes being made are for the purposes of authentic worship and not simply because we have a preference or appear out of touch or out of date or—God forbid—old fashioned? Do we know when to swallow our pride or bite our tongue (as the deacon did so well)? And even more critically important, how can we preserve the unity of the Spirit in the body when changes are necessary?

When there is a clash over worship styles, worship wars ensue. Dr. Charles Swindoll speaks directly and firmly to the issue of worship wars. "What God intended for His glory and for our corporate and personal growth—worship—has been transformed from a soul-deep commitment to an ugly, carnal fight," says Swindoll. "When any man- made tradition or expression of worship—old or new—is held on equal par with the Scriptures, we have gone too far. When we demand our own tradition—be it one of music . . . you name it—the requirement we insist on results in nothing less than legalism . . . If there is anything that brings delight to Satan, it is the disruption of the worship of God."[14]

A proper approach in developing the sounds of worship starts with an understanding that we are talking not so much about music, musicians, sound, or the mechanics of sound. Rather, we are looking, as Matt Redman[15] refers to so profoundly, to "the heart of the worship." If church staff, leaders, musicians, and volunteers do not have a clear, biblically centered concept of authentic worship, then all the rest is all for nothing. Without a biblically informed and guided view, leaders will follow a worldly perspective by default.

Swindoll summarizes the "wars and rumors of wars" issue superbly when he says, "What we want to cultivate in our churches: [is] not a group of selfish people who come together to be entertained, but a body of selfless believers who are learning how to worship God as a lifestyle."[16]

Question: Are you more interested in promoting your preferences for how worship should be conducted than seeking what our Lord desires and requires? Do you have a desire to cultivate the authentic worship of God as a lifestyle?

Chapter 2

Cultic Sounds

The "cult of sound" in worship is when we worship and make idols of the sound(s) we make, whether it be the sound of our voice, an instrument played, the mixed sound, or the technology that enhances sound, rather than worshiping the creator of sound.

"And the Lord said: '[These] people draw near with their mouth and honor me with their lips, while their hearts are far from me, and their fear of me is a commandment taught by men" (Isaiah 29:13).

"I am the Lord; that is my name; my glory I give to no other, nor my praise to carved idols" (Isaiah 42:8).

"For they exchanged the truth of God for a lie and worshiped and served the creature rather than the Creator, who is blessed forever. Amen" (Romans 1:25 NASB).

A "Christian" Concert

As previously mentioned, I served for a time in a church in Livermore, California. Soon after the church moved into a newly constructed building, one of the church members (a professional promoter) volunteered to promote and produce big-name Christian concerts at the church. Most church members were ecstatic about the possibilities. Professional concerts would give us a venue to hear artists we normally would not hear in person. The program was a huge success. Most of the concerts were sold out or nearly so. For the most part, I was fortunate to perform sound design and FOH for these events.

One of the groups brought in for a Saturday evening concert was a nationally known Christian "rock" band and selected to attract the youth of the city. A huge crowd of kids showed up that evening. Many were not Christian. But I am getting ahead of the story. The first indication that this concert was going to be different was when I was told I was not going to lead the sound team or perform FOH. The band hired a Bay-area (San Francisco Bay Area) sound engineer whom they knew and trusted. The sound had to be perfect, of course. The equalizations, the compressors, the levels, the mix, had to match the band's recorded sound. As I remember, the hired FOH was an incredibly talented engineer. I was happy to let him and his team handle the complexities of the band. From the start, the complications were manifold.

As soon as the band members arrived, it was obvious they were in a foul mood. They were tired from the road trip and hungry. And they let everyone know. When the band and crew entered the sanctuary, no greetings, introductions, or pleasantries were offered. All went straight to work. While setting up, the band complained about being fed only pizza and soda and voiced demands and complaints about the set-up.

The hired sound team struggled for a bit to meet the demand, while the band demonstrated little to no patience. The drummer couldn't hear the lead vocal. The electric guitar was not loud enough. The bass player complained that he did not "feel" the drum kick or his bass thumps. The scene was not unlike the complaining of the Children of Israel as they wandered in the wilderness.

Before long, the bickering and complaining transitioned from complaints about the sound to criticism of the band members, one to another. The theatrics consumed the afternoon and the entire rehearsal time. The rehearsal ended early when band members stormed off stage. From what I remember, they did not talk to each other until showtime.

The event was promoted as a nationally known band performing Christian songs as a witness to the youth of our city, and I wondered how the band could witness if their hearts were not right. How could they have compassion and love for the lost youth of Livermore if they didn't have compassion and love for each other and the fellow servants working with them? To paraphrase First Corinthians 13, no matter the capability or extreme talent I may possess, unless I love, I am just making a lot of useless noise.

When the band came on stage, the house was nearly packed. The expressions on the faces of the band members made it clear from the start that the band was still grousing, grumbling, and not the least bit happy. They played their song sets. The kids jumped out of their seats and rushed into the stage to dance and jump to the music. It was a Saturday night concert, and they were having fun. Near the end of the concert, the bandleader paused to talk to the crowd. He talked about Jesus and the salvation that comes from a right relationship to Him (though there was not a lot of joy on his face). As I sat in the sound booth, I thought the whole scene odd. Some kids responded. After talking to counselors, a few made a decision for Christ, and He receives the glory for lives surrendered to the Lord. The miracle of salvation was not odd. What was strange was that the bandleader could seamlessly offer an invitation while being out of fellowship with the band members and workers in the room.

Worshiping in Vain

> *Jesus said, "Well did Isaiah prophesy of you hypocrites, as it is written, 'This people honor me with their lips, but their heart is far from me; in vain do they worship me, teaching as doctrines the commandments of men.' You leave the commandment of God and hold to the tradition of men."* (Mark 7:6–8)

In this passage, Mark chronicles a typical scene from the Gospels. The Pharisees are up to their usual shenanigans, challenging Jesus. They charge His disciples with breaking the law when they do not wash their hands before eating. Jesus uses the opportunity (as He does all opportunities) for a critical teaching moment. He quotes Isaiah, "Their heart is far from me." The Pharisees believe they are honoring God, but they are not. They are worshiping themselves.

When we follow a sinful pattern of the world with our arguing and grousing, we worship ourselves, our stuff, our sounds, and our attitudes. Jesus says that type of worship is not a heart dedicated to Him and therefore in vain and useless. To be blunt, I believe most of the evening concert was "in vain" and useless before the Lord.

"But where sin abounded, grace did much more abound."[1] God is a gracious, loving God whose mercies and patience are without end. In the same manner that God was compassionate to the "stiff-necked" complaining children of Israel in the desert,

God demonstrated His graciousness that evening. Some youth responded. Some came to know salvation. In retrospect, most missed the blessing of fully serving the Lord with joy that Saturday evening. I wonder if the band would have had greater kingdom impact had they worshiped Christ that night instead of themselves.

Paul says in his letter to the Philippians, "Rejoice in the Lord always; again I will say, rejoice."[2] Paul wrote the letter to the Philippians while being imprisoned in ancient Rome's Mamertine prison. The prison is not far from the famous Colosseum. I can imagine while Paul was in prison, he could hear the activities taking place not that far from where he was. At times, Christians were being put to death as a spectator sport, yet Paul doesn't mention it. He doesn't publish articles against Emperor Nero. He doesn't complain about his unjust imprisonment. No! Rather than grouse and complain, Paul says, "Rejoice, again I say, rejoice."

No worship service, no event, compares to the monumental problems and challenges Paul faced. None. Yet Paul was able to say in the worst possible situation—facing execution for his faith—"Rejoice." Be glad. I believe his statements are intended to hit us like a two-by-four to the back of the head. Wake up. Nothing is important enough in sound or music for us to lose joy.

We may get discouraged. We may be disappointed. The sound mix may be terrible. A musician may play the wrong notes. A singer may be off-key. The FOH may miss a cue or ruin the mix. Rejoice in the midst of it. Rejoice and be glad. Worship is about Him, not us. We are imperfect creatures. He does not expect perfection. Rather, He expects our presence and participation in worshiping Him and glorifying Him above all others. The power of the Holy Spirit is given to us to be transformed and made new, constantly, even during our screwups.

Choosing to worship authentically involves a willingness to abandon the cult of our sounds and technology to be free to worship our Creator in the manner He requires. The Lord has gifted us, and we must be available to give our best gifts, talents, abilities, and skills in service to the Creator while being admonished to worship Him and not ourselves and our abilities. I want to explore further the use of our gifts and how they apply practically to sound for worship. Before I explore the mechanics, the question arises, what is worship—and more importantly, what is authentic worship within the context of making sound? What is it that truly brings glory and honor to our Lord and Savior? In the next section, I will explore authentic worship and how our decisions about sound and tech may affect our authenticity. I will also explore the attitudes leaders and servants should possess as we engage in worship together.

Questions: Have you been involved in or experienced the kind of bickering and fighting among band members and crew that follows the example in this chapter? Has it happened on a Sunday morning during worship? How did you feel about the lack of harmony? What did you do about it? How would you respond in the future if this kind of discord takes place?

PART II

Stewardship

Stewardship is the responsible overseeing and protection of something considered worth caring for and preserving.[1] Generally, we think of stewardship as our tithing and giving responsibilities and our attitudes about the stuff that God has given us for day-to-day living. In the context of *The Sounds of Worship*, stewardship should be viewed in its entirety. God has called each of us to a greater responsibility than tithing and giving.

In Genesis 1, God squarely plants the responsibility for dominion over all the earth with Adam and his offspring. We are also responsible for all the commandments of Jesus. He said, "If you love me you will keep my commandments."[2] Loving Jesus is loving His commandments in thought and deed. A faithful steward intentionally keeps God's commands.

If you are technical or musical or both and believe that theology is not for you, I urge you not to skip over this section. This chapter has relevant information that demonstrates that we all are worshipers, and all are responsible for the practice of worship. In this chapter, I will explain how the theology of worship directly impacts how we perform worship. I would also encourage you not to shrink from theological studies. Karl Barth once said, *"Every Christian must be a theologian."*

Chapter 3

Authentic Worship

"Worship is the supreme and only indispensable activity of the Christian Church. It alone will endure, like the love of God which it expresses, into heaven when all other activities of the Church will have passed away. It must therefore, even more strictly than any of the less essential doings of the Church, come under the criticism and control of the revelation on which the Church is founded" (W. Nichols, Jacob's Ladder).

"Worship isn't God's show. God is the audience. God's watching. The congregation, they are the actors in this drama. Worship is their show. And the minister is just reminding the people of their forgotten lines" (Soren Kierkegaard).

"Worship isn't primarily about music, techniques, songs, or methodologies. It's about what and who we love more than anything" (Bob Kauflin).

Begin with the End in Mind

One of Stephen Covey's core principles in the *Seven Habits of Highly Effective People* is "Begin with the end in mind."[1] Covey teaches that when we set out in life on any venture, we must first understand where we are headed. That principle is rooted in the Bible and is at work when Paul taught us to run the race with the end in mind.

> *Do you not know that in a race all the runners run, but only one receives the prize? So run that you may obtain it.* (1 Corinthians 9:24)

Paul compares the life of a Christian to a physical race. In his day, the race would have been on foot. Barefoot. To run a race (barefoot!) and win, one had to be intentionally in good shape, both physically and emotionally. Paul says our faith is played out in life (e.g. the process of sanctification) in the same manner as a physical race. Therefore, run the race to win. Run to win the prize—the crown of eternal life. Don't just live life for the here and now. Be mindful of what you are doing and achieving in the long term. Be intentional. It's a marathon, not a sprint. Begin with the end in mind.

Jesus taught to begin with the end in mind by counting the cost of discipleship.

> *For which of you, desiring to build a tower, does not first sit down and count the cost, whether he has enough to complete it? Otherwise, when he has laid a foundation and is not able to finish, all who see it begin to mock him, saying, "This man began to build and was not able to finish."* (Luke 14:28-30)

Jesus instructs His would-be disciples to count the cost of discipleship before commitment. We are instructed to intentionally, not blindly, understand the total cost (all that will be required of us) before embarking on the road of discipleship. Otherwise, we may not be able to finish. *Begin with the end in mind.*

Beginning with the end in mind in the context of *The Sounds of Worship* is to begin with an understanding of authentic worship. It means that we intentionally provide an atmosphere of authenticity when we gather as a body to worship. Authentic worship places first things first by worshiping the Creator, rather than His creation.

Whether you serve as FOH, musician, or song leader, why should you be concerned about authentic worship? Isn't that the pastor's job? After all, he's trained for this kind of thing and can direct us in the endeavor. It's true. The pastor may have worked through the issues of authentic worship. He may have the topic well in hand. But I submit that he is not the only one that must wrestle with the issue.

I can honestly say that those with whom I associate, commune, and pray seldom discuss the topic of worship, let alone authentic worship. We have grown up with the assumption that the form of congregational worship we lead and participate in is what should be. Our conversations evolve to a greater degree around improvements, timing, technique, and flow. I have always been one to promote a more professional setting and work earnestly toward making sure that the form of worship is the best we have to offer.

Worship is more than the form, though, and it isn't just the pastor or the music leader that is charged with authentic worship. We all are. We are the body of Christ and are called by our Lord and Savior to worship in spirit and in truth. Unless we understand and follow the requirements of authentic worship, we will fail to worship in a manner pleasing to our Lord. We fail to worship authentically when we have not committed ourselves to prayer and Bible study. We fail as well if we are not properly rehearsed and understand fully what will take place in our worship services. We fail when we do not keep the end in mind as we purchase equipment, build systems, arrange music, and build principles and practices that we assume will glorify God.

To honor and glorify God, we must first understand what God requires of us to enter into worship. Unless we know the requirements of authentic worship, we may miss the work of the Holy Spirit. Worse yet, we may grieve (or offend) the Holy Spirit through an assumption that God will accept my offering because I am serious or attempting to be genuine—or as is too often the case, I showed up.

In the previous chapters, we covered a plethora of areas where we worship wrong and bringing dishonor to the kingdom. Once we understand the requirements of authentic, God-centered, God-pleasing worship, then we can frame our discussion about the work we do and how it fits biblically in supporting worship.

While worship is truly a universal, non-ceasing activity of every Christian (we worship at all times, unless we are sinning), the context of this book confines most thoughts to congregational worship, even though the examples may be more personal. So much has been written on the topic of worship that one would think there would be no further need for discussion on the matter. Yet the struggle to find authentic worship, as we have seen in previous chapters, is real. At times, seeking pure worship is not just a struggle but a fight! We struggle because of the increased number of distractions, not the least of which is the technology we use in modern worship and in our daily lives.

When Worship Becomes Real

> *In the year that King Uzziah died I saw the Lord sitting upon a throne, high and lifted up; and the train of his robe filled the temple. Above him stood the seraphim. Each had six wings: with two he covered his face, and with two he covered his feet, and with two he flew. And one called to another and said: "Holy, holy, holy is the Lord of hosts; the whole earth is full of his glory! And the foundations of the thresholds shook at the voice of him who called, and the house was filled with smoke. And I said: "Woe is me! For I am lost; for I am a man of unclean lips, and I dwell in the midst of a people of unclean lips; for my eyes have seen the King, the Lord of hosts!"* (Isaiah 6:1-5)

Isaiah's experience provides a provocative look into heaven in a scene that is a bit confusing. We are confronted with an overwhelming image of heavenly worship in the holiest place before Almighty God. This is an alien place filled with smoke and otherworldly creatures, the seraphim, worshiping God. Here, at this moment, Isaiah is overwhelmed by his sinful nature and the sin of his people. As he stands before the Almighty, all he can utter is, "Woe is me!"

Have you had a similar experience? Have you stood before the Almighty (perhaps not exactly as Isaiah) in prayer, in the presence of God? Have you then seen your abject poverty as a sinful creation before the Lord? The starting point for authentic worship is "Woe is me!" To be in a woeful state means that we see ourselves as sinners who have no justification for our sinful ways. The psalmist declares, "Worship the Lord in the splendor of holiness; tremble before him, all the earth!"[2] And the writer of

Hebrews declares, "Let us be grateful for receiving a kingdom that cannot be shaken, and thus let us offer to God acceptable worship, with reverence and awe, for our God is a consuming fire."[3]

Authentic worship starts when we see ourselves clearly as sinful creatures before a holy and righteous God. But the story does not stop there. God does not leave Isaiah in a woeful state.

> *Then one of the seraphim flew to me, having in his hand a burning coal that he had taken with tongs from the altar. And he touched my mouth and said: "Behold, this has touched your lips; your guilt is taken away, and your sin atoned for."* (Isaiah 6:6-7)

Isaiah's guilt is removed, and his sin atoned. God's grace in the forgiveness of our sin is commended to us in the same manner as it was to Isaiah. God responds to our acknowledged sinful state with redemption. We, like Isaiah, receive the removal of sin.

The beginning of authentic worship starts and continues with our recognizing that we are sinful creatures before God. We have violated His commands. We stand guilty of his judgment. We need forgiveness. We need a Savior who is worthy and able to forgive. At the same time, we are not left with the guilt of condemnation; we are raised up, and we experience this "glorious thought, my sin not in part but the whole, is nailed to the cross and I bear it no more. Praise the Lord, oh my soul."[4]

The psalmist writes,

> *One thing have I asked of the Lord, that will I seek after: that I may dwell in the house of the Lord all the days of*

> *my life, to gaze upon the beauty of the Lord and to inquire in his temple.* (Psalm 27:4)

Pastor and scholar Ligon Duncan says, "Worship is our enjoyment of Him. Our celebration of Him. It's something we get to do. Not something we have to do. It's not duty as much as it is delight."[5] Practicing and delighting in worship is for now, and it should be continuous and not just in a future idyllic place. We easily forget, as W. Nichols says, worship transcends all other activities of the body of Christ and will last forever. Nothing should get in the way.

Worship is placing the highest value on God

> *He [the Christ] is the image of the invisible God, the firstborn of all creation. For by him all things were created, in heaven and on earth, visible and invisible, whether thrones or dominions or rulers or authorities—all things were created through him and for him. And he is before all things, and in him all things hold together.* (Colossians 1:15-17)

St. Augustine declared, "You are sweeter than all pleasure, though not flesh and blood, you who outshine all light, yet are hidden deeper than any secret in our hearts, you who surpass all honor in themselves . . . O Lord, my God, my Wealth, and my Salvation."[6]

God is greater than our music, our technology, our egos, and our desire to be recognized and awarded for what we accomplish. Augustine says, "He loves thee too little who loves anything together with thee, which he loves not for thy sake."[7] In other words, if I love anything above God, or as much as God, then I love Him far too little. When I delight in my own abilities and accomplishments without seeing those abilities as coming solely from Him and are wholly and completely subject to Him, I form idols that blind me to authentic worship of the Creator. St. Augustine reminds us that "every moment in every circumstance we stand on the brink between the lure of idolatry and the delight of seeing and knowing God."[8] We become idolaters when we depend on technology to engage and move the congregation. We are idolaters when we act as though our skill in playing an instrument or performing a mix is what brings about the presence and movement of the Holy Spirit. We make idols of our talents and gifts and parade around in an elitist fashion. Anytime I entertain the idea that I am "better than," I have built an idol. Isaiah says that we honor the Sabbath when we desist from following our own ways, from seeking our pleasure, and from speaking our own words because we take delight in the Lord. (Isaiah 58:12).

Worshiping in "spirit and truth" stands in stark contrast to worship that is symbolic, or typical, or just showing up.[9] The acts of authentic worship call us to be intentional and prepared. Too often, we allow our service simply to flow. If we have been mixing or playing music or singing or leading for any length of time, the process can become rote, routine, predictable.

When was the last time you earnestly looked for and sought after the glory of God in your services? Did you see God's glory evident in the last worship service? It's not about our feelings and emotions; it's not about how well the service ran; it's not about how great the sermon was delivered; it's not about how many were in attendance. And it's not about nailing the mix, slamming home a solo, or a unique lick on the guitar. In contrast and more importantly, was our Lord and Savior Jesus Christ glorified through all that was done genuinely in my heart?

One of the purposes of writing this book is to help bridge the gaps and reduce wars between the ministerial staff and the technical staff and volunteers. We all approach this topic from a different perspective. The framework for our approach to worship is vastly and understandably different and depends on one's function and position. I am not a professional musician. When thinking and working through how a service will be conducted, I am thinking about the sound and media, and about wires, microphones (which one?), monitor, and house mix levels, etc.

The bandleader is thinking about the songs, how the music will be arranged, who will show up this Sunday to play, and what he must do to the arrangements if someone does not. The musicians are focused on their singing or playing and the notes and chords and making sure they can be heard. And the pastor is concerned about the sermon, the visitors, and the overall flow of the service. Our common ground is found in worship and the object of our worship. Our Lord and the call to worship Him is the starting point. Everything we do, all that we perform, should flow from and be subordinate to genuine, heartfelt worship.

Engaging with the Creator in authentic worship is the antidote for when I am tempted to be snarky because a guitar is not on the right chord or when someone is giving me a bad time about the mix. When I enter into worship with an attitude of joy, rather than "task" or personal gratification, I am able to see the Holy Spirit at work—not only in me but those around me. *Soli Deo Gloria* (to God alone be all glory now and forevermore).

The "Where of Worship"

> *The woman said to him, "Sir, I perceive that you are a prophet. Our fathers worshiped on this mountain, but*

you say that in Jerusalem is the place where people ought to worship." Jesus said to her, "Woman, believe me, the hour is coming when neither on this mountain nor in Jerusalem will you worship the Father. You worship what you do not know; we worship what we know, for salvation is from the Jews. But the hour is coming, and is now here, when the true worshipers will worship the Father in spirit and truth, for the Father is seeking such people to worship him. God is spirit, and those who worship him must worship in spirit and truth." (John 4:19-24)

If the truth be told, we seem stuck on the idea that worship only happens in certain venues with a certain kind of equipment. We are at times overly concerned with facilities and making sure those facilities are welcoming and modern. Yet Jesus talks about worship that transcends location and having a roof over our heads. Jesus makes it clear that the temple in Jerusalem would soon not be the place of worship that it had been for hundreds of years. Rather, Jesus points out that worshiping in spirit and in truth is not worship in a physical temple.

In the context of John 4, we are shown the blessing and the freedom to worship our Lord at any time, not being bound by walls and structure. The profound indwelling power of the Holy Spirit in both the body of Christ and in our bodies leads us in authentic worship at all times and in all places.

We have developed in our collective wisdom that we must have facilities with movable seating, a stage with lights, a great sound system (that rocks the house), and good HVAC, among many other requirements. If we are to take Jesus seriously, it makes no difference the kind of facilities we gather in—a school gymnasium, a rented theater, or a football field. When we engage and practice authentic worship and simply delight in Him and Him alone, the surroundings are superfluous.[10]

A Perfect Worship Service?

As we seek authentic worship, C.S. Lewis frames the topic for us well. He discusses the elements of a "perfect" worship service. I quote him at length.

> *"It looks as if they believed people can be lured to go to church by incessant brightenings, lightenings, lengthenings, abridgements, simplifications, and complications of the service. And it is probably true that a new, keen vicar will usually be able to form within his parish a minority who are in favour of his innovations. The majority, I believe, never are. Those who remain—many give up churchgoing altogether—merely endure.*
>
> *"Novelty, simply as such, can have only an entertainment value. And they don't go to church to be entertained. They go to use the service, or, if you prefer, to enact it. Every service is a structure of acts and words through which wereceive a sacrament, or repent, or supplicate, or adore. And it enables us to do these things best—if you like, it "works" best—when, through long familiarity, we don't have to think about it. As long as you notice, and have to count, the steps, you are not yet dancing but only learning to dance. A good shoe is a shoe you don't notice. Good reading becomes possible when you need not consciously think about eyes, or light, or print, or spelling.* ***The perfect church service would be one we were almost unaware of; our attention would***

> ***have been on God.*** *But every novelty prevents this. It fixes our attention on the service itself; and thinking about the worship is a different thing from worshipping...Tis mad idolatry that makes the service greater than the god."* [emphasis added][11]

C.S. Lewis has packed a great deal of wisdom in a rather short discussion on the topic of worship. His comments are as applicable today as they were in his day. Never mind that he is talking about the Anglican Church of England in the 1940s. This could be any modern church setting.

Church Order

In many churches, it has been fashionable not to publish the order of service.[12] By not committing to an order, we leave the possibility open for variations in the service that may leave some confused. Am I supposed to greet someone during the service this morning, or are we skipping that today? Will there be a closing benediction, or can I wander off during the last song, or does it matter? Do I stand during the offering or sit? I must sit, of course; otherwise, I can't pass the plate in an orderly fashion. But do I stand to join the singing of the offertory after the plate is passed or not?

Even worse, congregants may feel they can interrupt the service with something that is bothering them. When members believe that the worship service is like any other meeting time, the flow is disrupted and worshipers are distracted. God is not honored in the hearts of those whose focus on Him and has been displaced by something that is irrelevant to the service.

If it's not written down, congregants will not know the script to follow and not know what is expected of them and when. Band members can get confused and not be ready because of last minute changes. And the poor FOH must determine "on the fly" whose microphone should be open and when. Does it make sense that our services are prepared and ordered in a form that we are almost unaware of? Like wearing a good fitting shoe? And orderly?

Authentic Worship Is Relevant to All Ages

As discussed in Chapter 1 of this book, for the first time in history, six generations live side-by-side. Each generation, depending upon when they were born, has their own style, identity, and preferences for how they live, what they wear, what music they listen to, and what core values they will live by and promote. We have all experienced the different attitudes on dating, sex, drug abuse, politics, work, and play. Each generation defends their perspective as being correct and normal. Sadly, the evangelical church of America has allowed those generational differences to define how we are to worship. Unfortunately, those differences are at the heart of worship wars.

There are no scriptural mandates, requirements, commands, or admonishments to separate ourselves by age so that we can enjoy worship in the manner that suits us best. In fact, Scripture states the opposite.

> *Likewise, teach the older women to be reverent in the way they live, not to be slanderers or addicted to much wine, but to teach what is good. Then they can urge the younger women to love their husbands and children, to be self-controlled and pure, to be busy at home, to be*

> *kind, and to be subject to their husbands, so that no one will malign the word of God.* (Titus 2:3-5 NIV)

How will the older generation impart the wisdom of the ages to the younger generations if they do not stand together in the same worship? How will each generation learn to trust the other if all are not fellowshipping with each other? How will the younger children understand and know how to participate in worship if they are segregated to their own age group? Why would teens want to join adults in worship if they have been fed a steady diet of youth-focused messages and music? How can we be one if we are constantly separating ourselves from each other based on age or preference?

There is simply no biblical basis to withhold worship based on my personal preference and desires no matter the age. The body of Christ cuts through all differences. Paul provides clear instruction to be "one in Christ."

> *There is neither Jew nor Greek, there is neither slave nor free, there is no male and female, for you are all one in Christ Jesus.* (Galatians 3:28)

The church has a wonderful challenge and responsibility to bring together all disciples of Christ, no matter the age, into one unifying, cross-generational praise and worship of our Lord. To do otherwise is to completely ignore our mandate: "by this all men will know that you are My disciples—if you have love for one another" (John 13:35 NASB). Obeying the commandment means that we intentionally plan how we order the content, music, and teaching moments of our worship services.

Sing New Songs

On a recent coast-to-coast trip, I was struck by a flight attendant's pedantic repetition of the flight safety rules and requirements. The scenario is presented the same every time prior to takeoff and landing with only small variations to add color. We are reminded to fasten our seatbelts and shown how to do it, even though nearly all of the passengers already know how to do it. In fact, most passengers could most likely recite Southwest Airlines Safety Briefing, Chapter 1 verses 1 through 6 verbatim.

1:1 In preparation for takeoff,

1:2 Please place all carryon luggage either in the overhead bins or completely stowed under the seat in front of you. If you are not able to stow your luggage, please ring the flight attendant button, and an attendant will check your baggage for you at no charge.

1:3 Buckle your seat belts by inserting one end into the clasp and place it low across your waist. Please remain seated with your belt fastened during the flight unless the captain turns off the seatbelt sign.

1:4 In preparation for takeoff, please place your seats and tray tables in their fully upright and locked position.

1:5 Turn off all computers and stow them safely either under the seat in front of you or in the overhead bin.

1:6 Place all portable devices into airplane mode or game mode before takeoff.

1:7 In the unlikely event that we lose cabin pressure, three oxygen masks will drop down. If you are traveling with a small child, or someone acting like a small child, place the mask on first before placing it on the child. Breath normally. Oxygen will flow normally even if the bag does not inflate.

I particularly enjoy the phrase, "In the unlikely event . . ."

Though I have heard these instructions hundreds of times over the years, no flight attendant says, "You all look like seasoned travelers and already know the routine. For brevity and to avoid boring you to death and interrupting the particularly important time with your phone, I won't remind you of these important flight instructions that just might save your life." Or "Please raise your hand if you need to know the safety instructions, and maybe we can meet after the flight to discuss it in more detail." And I have never heard a passenger say, "Do we really have to go through all this again? We all know it. Let's get this plane in the air." Or "Come on! I've flown thousands of times. Tell me something I don't know."

The fact is, we require reminding! FAA rules require that we be reminded through the pedantic repetition of the same information on every leg of every flight. Pay attention. Though it may be the same old "song," your life depends on it.

Sometimes we enjoy being reminded of an old song, which can be illustrated with a modern phenomenon, the classic movie. One of my favorites, *A Wonderful Life,* with Jimmy Stewart and Donna Reed, is a classic that I can view over and over without being bored or distracted. I know every scene and most lines of the movie. I know when George Bailey is going to have goodness in his life and when it goes south. I know the parts where he is frustrated and angry, and where he smiles and sings with Mary, "Buffalo Bill won't you come out tonight, come out tonight, come out tonight . . . (then slowly) and dance by the light of the moon." I can quote on cue, "Our teacher says every time a bell rings, an angel gets his wings." The movie tells a magical, timeless tale of the perseverance of good in the face of a persistent (and at times overarching) evil.

Most of us have a favorite movie (or more than one) that we can watch repeatedly and never tire of the plot line, the acting, the characters, or the ending. Even if we know the surprise ending and all the twists in between, we still watch it with some anticipation and satisfaction. We may even have key lines memorized and repeat them on cue. We laugh at the same jokes and may cry at the same sad scenes. Each time we watch our favorite movie, we are, though we know all the details of the story, conscientiously determining to experience it as though it were the first time. Familiarity with the content is not a deterrent.

We are encouraged in the Word to remember the commands of God through repetition.

> *These words that I command you today shall be on your heart. You shall teach them diligently to your children, and shall talk of them when you sit in your house, and when you walk by the way, and when you lie down, and when you rise. You shall bind them as a sign on your hand, and they shall be as frontlets between your eyes. You shall write them on the doorposts of your house and on your gates.* (Deuteronomy 6:6-9)

Why do you need to write them down and teach them and remember them? Because "your very life depends on them!"[13]

Yet we live in a culture that values constant, and at times

tiresome, change. Out with the old, in with the new. We feed on a diet of fresh, new, exciting ideas, whether it be fashion, lifestyle, or business. As evangelicals, we have allowed the cultural groupthink to permeate our thinking. We demand new and fresh music and programs. The groupthink says that if we repeat the old forms of worship, we may become stale or antiquated or (God forbid) out-of-touch. A common proof text for "new" is from David's declaration, "Sing to the Lord a new song."[14] Both Isaiah 42:10 and Psalm 33:3 begin with similar messages: "Sing to the Lord a new song" and "Sing to him a new song." Psalm 144:9 declares, "I will sing a new song to you, O God."

All too often, the conventional interpretation of "Sing a new song" revolves around stylistic and cultural change. According to Dr. Harold Best, that is precisely what David is not talking about. He is calling on the worshipers to sing each song (old, new, or tired) as though it were new, not necessarily different. Sing it with fresh eyes and heart, and not as rote or ritual. Best puts it this way, "We can sing a truly new song only once, and thereafter we repeat it . . . Singing a song newly means that we must sing the thousandth repetition as if for the first time."[15]

A new song is anti-ritualistic. "When ritual is performed over and over again, it becomes an old song. Emphasizing that the psalm is a new one means that it is not ritual. It is pure glorification, pure praise directed towards God, not some old mechanical routine that worshipers perform for the sake of gaining credit with their fellow men"[16] or with God.

As we enter worship, we hear stories that we have heard before, sometimes over and over all our life. Many of the stories we know by heart in the same manner as we hear flight instructions over and over or have favorite movies we watch over and over.

We are called to sing songs we have sung before, some that we may sing as rote. Yet each time we hear and each time we sing, we are to sing with fresh voices and hear with fresh awareness of and thankfulness to our Lord and Savior. We remember the story. We repeat the story. We rejoice in the telling, listening, and singing of the story. His story. That is what David meant by "sing a new song."

Quite some time ago, I was tuning through cable channels (as I used to be in the habit of doing) looking for something to capture my attention. I stopped on a locally produced program on a Christian television station. The program featured a local pastor and his wife, talking about everything one could imagine. They were both very handsome and had good stage presence. The show presumably was to promote the church where the host was pastor, but much of it centered solely on the personalities of the host and hostess. I cannot say I was interested.

While I did not find my soul being fed, I painfully stuck with it because Joni Eareckson Tada was the guest. When Joni was introduced, she talked about a deep, abiding faith that had developed in her life as a result of being severely handicapped. She talked of a walk with the Lord that made my walk seem superficial and mediocre by comparison. During the interview, it was clear that the pastor and especially his wife did not understand. The wife asked frivolous questions about clothing, makeup, and other nonsensical topics. Joni was more than patient navigating the small talk, but then she said, "When you have nowhere to go but flat on your face for hours at a time every single day, you have an opportunity to truly know God." I gave her statement a lot of thought. Is there an advantage to being handicapped[17] in such a manner that prompts worship rather than boredom or madness?

I think about it today and as I write this, I think about Joni being in exactly the same place day after day, "flat on her face" with nowhere to go and nothing to entertain her. There, in that same, never changing, difficult place—the same old song—Joni says she finds authentic worship, truly knowing God and demonstrates the essence of singing a new song.

In Revelation 21:5 Jesus proclaims, "Behold, I am making all things new." Designed into the creation and the future of the creation are events and moments that we will experience over and over. While we experience similar or same events over and over, we experience them all in new and fresh ways. He is continually making all things new—no cloud is ever the same, no sunset, no rain, no sunrise. All are made new. He does not have to change the components of the experience to make it new. He simply allows us to discover different aspects, nuances, and pleasure from what would be otherwise mundane. And He receives all the glory.

Singing old songs as new includes being reminded: that we are sinners saved by grace; that it is by the mercy of God that Christ provided a once-and-for-all sacrifice for our sin; that He was resurrected on the third day and lives eternally; that Jesus is the only way, truth, and life; and that no one comes to the Father but by Him (John 14:6). By grace we are saved and not of ourselves. How many times do we need reminders of the old song of salvation? Daily! How often should we be reminded of the tenets of our faith as a church? Every time we worship. When we repeat the fundamental truths of our salvation, we are acknowledging that those truths are life. Our lives depend on them!

Singing old songs as new is an antidote for being caught up in what is trendy or a fad or simply culturally significant. The practice brings simplicity, not complexity to worship. Singing old songs as new keeps us focused on the reason why we are gathering to worship. After all, we are worshiping the Ancient of Days. He is the same yesterday, today, and tomorrow (Hebrews 13:8). He never changes.

There are times for professional music teams to show what they can do. There are times when a new style and trendy music is suitable. But those times may not be appropriate on Sunday morning. Worship should not be the time when I am entertained or guessing what is coming next. As C.S. Lewis says, worship should be like a "good-fitting shoe."[18]

Cutting Through Superficiality

God desires to cut through our superficial notions of worship—of style, newness for newness' sake, emotional highs, and manipulation—and be brought back to the fundamentals. An attitude of authentic worship requires absolute honesty before the Lord and a willingness to accept His response. Authentic worship is not about an emotion, a high, or a feel-good moment. It is not self-help (or Jesus help) therapy.[19]

Worship is not about me feeling better about myself. Rather, authentic worship happens when we are laid bare before the Lord with no excuses, nothing between Him and us. Then and only then are we able to receive the full measure of His unfailing, never-ending mercy, and His unmerited, underserved grace.

Anytime humans are involved, results are less than perfect, but perhaps we needn't strive for perfection as it may interfere with the work of the Holy Spirit. Authenticity in worship is not about achieving a perfectly executed service, e.g., no errors in delivery of sermon, all musicians in perfect key and time, and no distractions or mistakes. Instead, it is about allowing, facilitating, and encouraging an individual's worship blended with the whole of the body along with our imperfectness, flaws, and mess-ups. Authentic worship is when believers are wholly and completely in the presence of God, worshiping Him and Him alone, prompted by words and music, and encouraged and lifted up by the worship of those around them.

Questions: Have you prayed about and sought authentic worship of our Lord and Savior in your personal life? Has this chapter prompted you to think differently about your role in congregational worship? Are you willing to make the necessary changes to bring the spirit of authentic worship to your congregation? What would have to change?Additional questions: Does the idea of worship being a good-fitting shoe, as Lewis says, bother you? Do you feel the need for something new and exciting every service? Are you dependent upon gimmicks, stage props, lightings, etc., in order to perform worship and make it relevant to the culture? What are the criteria for you to have participated in a successful time of worship?

Worship Disrupters and How to Handle Them

I grew up in the church. I come from a family of teachers, pastors, professors, and leaders who taught and disciplined me in worship for my entire life. Thinking back, I remember at the earliest age being in worship with my family, grandparents, aunts, and uncles. In those days, children were expected to sit with their family. I remember struggling to sit still and pretending to pay attention. Children's church wasn't around in those days. It wasn't even imagined. The tone of the services was always solemn and reverential.

My kind grandmother took mercy on my siblings and me at an early age. She would faithfully bring paper and pen or pencil and encourage us to sit on the floor between pews, or even under the pew, and doodle. As we grew older, though, we were expected to sit and listen quietly. Those rules did not deter us from finding diversions. We passed notes back and forth; sometimes the notes were sneaked between the rows.

When we were caught, the looks, the talking to, the punishment was usually severe. However, I remember something interesting about an attitude honed over the years of not paying attention. It was cool if you could send notes back and forth or even communicate with soft whispers or crude sign language and not get caught.

As I grew older, I never lost the idea that while others had to listen, I could get away with not paying attention. My siblings and friends felt the same way at times. While our parents insisted that we needed to pay attention, we rebelled and acted as though we really didn't have to.

I wonder if there's something similar happening today not just with kids but primarily with adults. I wonder if we see ourselves above it all and don't have to listen and keep quiet if we don't feel like it. Given our busy lifestyles, we may have something far more important to attend to. We might receive a text message from a friend to which we feel we must respond. We may feel the need to check the latest social media posts. We might have an "important" phone call we need to receive or to make. We may even come to service fashionably late and then act frustrated that no one has left a row open for us. While a row might be completely open in the front, the Lord knows we're not going to sit there (especially in a Baptist church).

Senior adults may gather in groups during the last song of the service and talk loud above the music to plan where they are headed for lunch. Someone may talk and visit during the offertory. Individuals may interrupt the pastor before the sermon or during the sermon to ask an irrelevant question or make a personal statement they believe everyone needs to hear. Some people take phone calls in the middle of service and carry on the conversation while the pastor is preaching.

And then there is the food. Some people believe if they are hungry or thirsty, getting up in the middle of the service to replenish their cookie plate or coffee cup is perfectly okay. While this may sound unbelievable, some people show up for worship with their own musical instruments to play with the band.[20]

The disruption can also come from the staff or worship team. A guitar player may insist on a nuanced lick he has just learned and want to parade it in front of the congregation or significant other. A singer may sing in a manner that shows off their voice but does nothing to help the congregation sing the song. An FOH may be frustrated with a member of the band and decide to turn the band member's instrument off (or turn it down so low it can barely be heard). A worship leader may make fun of something that has gone wrong with the service and cause humiliation to those involved.

Then some distractions just happen—not from individuals acting in an impertinent manner, but when something goes awry accidently. Like a guitar string snapping. Or the power going out. Or someone tripping on the way to the pulpit. Or a baby crying. Whatever the reason for the disruption, these situations interrupt the natural flow of worship and cause a discontinuity.

For all involved, disruptions can be so severe that congregants may struggle or never get back to authentic worship.

Several strategies can help remove or least reduce the distractions. For the disrupters that come from the congregation, I suggest that each church (the local body of Christ), take the time to determine how to best handle the congregants who interrupt the worship service.

For worship leaders and staff, a good exercise would be to determine as a group what is fitting and right for worship.[21] For instance, should band members play or singers sing in a manner that the congregation cannot follow?[22] Is this kind of playing ever appropriate? What is appropriate clothing? Are certain outfits too provocative or simply inappropriate for a God-honoring time of worship?

Take some time to observe what the band members and sound team are doing during the welcome, announcements, and prayer time. Are they whispering to each other? On their phones? Are they off in their own world practicing the next song? When the worship team is focused on anything other than worship and facilitating worship, they give the impression that the music is worship, or at the least, it is the most important part of the service. Everyone is performing in worship, not just band members.

When disruptions occur due to disagreements or hurt feelings between worship team members, the leadership must take the responsibility and the time to resolve the disharmony prior to worship! Everyone on the worship team must be in harmony with one another. Any bickering or bitterness that crosses into the time of congregational worship poisons the work of the Holy Spirit.

Questions: How would you handle disruptions to the worship service that are coming from the congregation? What situations demand that you act immediately? Or would you wait and use the opportunity as a teaching opportunity for those involved? How would you handle worship team members that insist their talents be put on display? Is there room for a band member to show their talent during a worship service.

Chapter 4

Professionalism and Performance

"I will play music before the Lord. And I will be even more undignified than this, and will be humble in my own sight" (2 Samuel 6:21-22 NKJV).

"The sacrifices of God are a broken spirit; a broken and contrite heart, O God, you will not despise" (Psalm 51:17).

"For by the grace given to me I say to everyone among you not to think of himself more highly than he ought to think, but to think with sober judgment, each according to the measure of faith that God has assigned" (Romans 12:3).

It's Sunday Morning Again!

The Sunday morning setup for worship went well. Rehearsal was better than usual, and the band and tech team felt confident they were ready for the worship service. When the first note of the first song was struck, however, a musician was in the wrong key. The worship leader stopped and counted off a new beginning. The congregation waited. This time two band members were in the wrong key and everyone else was correct.

Again, the worship leader stopped and started again. And again, for the third time, the music was restarted. This time, only one instrument was out of key, and the band played on. What happened next surprised all. The congregation, knowing the song and knowing it well, sang strong and brought the band along. The congregation cued and carried the band. The rest of the music was played without misstep, and the small congregational singing could be heard some distance away.

After the service, some of the band members were upset with the others for making such a simple mistake, and some feelings were hurt that they looked bad before the church. Amid God's gracious gift, giving all an opportunity to perform before Him, some missed the point and missed what really happened.

One of my college art professors used to compare western documentary artists C. M. Russell and Frederic Remington. My professor preferred Russell to Remington all day long and encouraged me to study him. I did and produced a video documentary on the life of C.M. Russell. Not many appreciate Russell's gritty, realistic style. One of his paintings in particular, *Waiting for a Chinook,* seems minimalist in style. It's more of a sketch than a painting. Nevertheless, the scene is an emaciated cow barely standing in sub-zero snow while waiting for the salvation of a warm chinook. At the same time, this sad looking cow is surrounded by a wolf pack, salivating for a meal. I have never forgotten the painting. It's seared into my mind. It's gritty and it's real.

Russell's body of work stands in stark contrast to Remington's. When Remington painted the cavalry, according to my professor, "Every piece of accoutrement was perfectly in place." Neither Remington nor Russell would be considered unprofessional nor unworthy of consideration. There is a place for both, but for the purposes of discussion, I want to side with Russell's body of work and his style. I identify with Russell. My work, my art, my designs, are not always the prettiest. My work is gritty at times, but hopefully genuine and from the heart.

Sometimes, not everything comes together as we would like or as we think it should be. Let's face it, most musicians and sound team members in churches today are not professionals and are largely self-taught. Not every piece of accruement is perfectly in place. Nevertheless, even when professionals are present, mistakes are made. Cues are missed. Not all comes together seamlessly. Though we fail and at times fall flat on our faces, the Lord is gracious and merciful to us. *He is jealous for our worship* even when we struggle in our performance.

Heartfelt and Genuine

Being genuine, as taught in Scripture, transcends how we are viewed by others. It is far more important than image. When Jesus compared the Pharisee's prayer to that of the sinner, He gave us a parable that can smack us between the eyes like a two-by-four. He also told this parable to some who trusted in themselves that they were righteous, and treated others with contempt:

> *Two men went up into the temple to pray, one a Pharisee and the other a tax collector. The Pharisee, standing by himself, prayed thus: 'God, I thank you that I am not like other men, extortioners, unjust, adulterers, or even like this tax collector. I fast twice a week; I give tithes of all that I get.' But the tax collector, standing far off, would not even lift up his eyes to heaven, but beat his breast, saying, 'God, be merciful to*

me, a sinner!' I tell you, this man went down to his house justified, rather than the other. For everyone who exalts himself will be humbled, but the one who humbles himself will be exalted. (Luke 18:9-14)

A famous director of a well-known music conservatory tells the story of looking for a new church home after retiring and moving to a new city. In his quest, he explored many churches. His criteria for a church home was two-fold. The preaching had to be Bible centric, and the music needed to match his perception of excellence.

After visiting many churches, he found the music in some to be amateurish and lacking, while in others, he found a preciseness and excellence in the music performances. When asked which church he selected as his new home, he said he picked one that was less precise in their execution of the music. The reason? When the musicians performed, he felt the heart of worship more in those playing who made mistakes and errors than in those who played perfectly.

We may think God is only glorified when the service is perfect or near perfect. Is it possible that a service can go terribly awry, terribly bad (from a human perspective), with missed cues on music, songs played in the wrong chord, missed microphone mutes, a prayer that talked more about self than God, and yet still God is glorified?

Perhaps it's time to stop worrying what others think about my music, my mix, or my phenomenal collection of bleeding-edge equipment and effects, and instead focus on what God thinks. Am I honoring Him with all that I do?

Professionalism in worship means that I am honoring Him by being prepared and intentional, knowing who I am performing for, and understanding my place in worship.

Being prepared means that I am primarily and foremost spiritually prepared and then both musically and technically prepared. It means that I have studied the Bible and prayed for the service and for others in the service.

Being intentional means the service is planned, and all involved know the plan and have rehearsed the plan.

When I know and understand who the audience for my performance is, I realize that the service is not about me. Bob Goff wrote, "Next time you're tempted to boast [about your great ability, skill, or talent], just say under your breath, 'It's not about me.' Say it a dozen times a day. Say it a thousand times a month. Say it when you bless a meal or do something wonderful or selfless or when you help hurting people. Make it your anthem."[1]

> *Do nothing out of selfish ambition or vain conceit, but in humility consider others better than yourselves. Each of you should look not only to your own interests, but also to the interests of others.* (Philippians 2:3-4)

Professionalism also means that when things do not work as expected, I continue the best I can, mistakes and all, realizing I am honoring God in the process.

Professionalism and My Attitude Towards Others

"I'm an Audio Engineer. For the sake of argument, let's assume I am never wrong."[2]

Professionalism in worship extends to how I treat others and especially those within the body. Jesus said that all men will know His disciples by their love for one another. As you perform, are others respected? Do you demonstrate honor to those around you? If you are in a position of authority, do you assume you know all aspects of music, tech, and worship, or do you work as a team with each person contributing in each area of expertise?

The assumptions we make are sometimes laughable, especially when we make those assumptions outside of our area of giftedness and expertise. As I am writing this book, the great genius of the last few hundred years has passed away. Stephen Hawking, the English theoretical physicist, cosmologist, author, and Director of Research at the Centre for Theoretical Cosmology within the University of Cambridge has left a large hole in the cadre of the elite community of theoretical scientists.

Hawking theorized on the existence of black holes and built a computational model that demonstrated that radiation is emitted from a black hole. According to many, he should have received the Nobel Prize for his work. Hawking did not. Not because he was underserving, but because scientists have yet to observe in reality what Hawking says exists in theory. In his area of expertise, Hawking lived in the stratosphere of geniuses and has few equals.

Stephen Hawking was an atheist. He argued and wrote about the nonexistence of God. In one of his final publications, *The Grand Design,* he argues that the existence of gravity is proof that God does not exist. "Because there is a law such as gravity, the universe can and will create itself from nothing. Spontaneous creation is the reason there is something rather than nothing, why the universe exists, why we exist. It is not necessary to invoke God to light the blue touch paper and set the universe going."[3]

Is Steven Hawking credible? Is he persuasive? Is he compelling? Yes, yes, and yes. Few people on the planet have as much credibility as Hawking. Considering his expertise, his compelling and credible statements, how is it that a theoretical cosmologist knows for certain that God does not exist?

Hawking, according to those close to him, studied little philosophy and did not read the Bible. How is it that he feels compelled to make such grand, overarching statements without knowing what the Bible has to say? And what the Creator of the universe has to say about him? The simple fact is, Hawking knows nothing of the Creator of the universe and nothing about His existence.

Stephen Hawking is an excellent example of a person who routinely made profound but untrue statements. Even the most gifted and well-known people step outside their areas of expertise with claims that their expertise in one area makes them an expert in other areas of life. Richard Feynman, the famous mathematician and winner of the Nobel Prize in physics said, "I believe that a scientist looking at nonscientific problems is just as dumb as the next guy—and when he talks about a nonscientific matter, he sounds as naive as anyone untrained in the matter."[4] I applaud Feynman's honesty.

In the body of Christ, we fall flat on our face professionally and fail to understand the gifts of the Spirit when we assume we know and can direct in areas outside our expertise or giftedness or skill base. An FOH who studies sound design, acoustics, equalization, etc., may be expert in those areas but may know little to nothing about playing an instrument. A musician who is accomplished at their art with years of training and playing may know nothing about how to mic the instrument or how to achieve a natural sound in a venue. A pastor may not want to fix the acoustics in his sanctuary due to the prohibitive costs but may rather communicate that the church doesn't need any improvement. In these three cases, a little information about the other discipline can create an even greater degree of disconnect. All should understand professionalism applies to more than skill and abilities. In the body of Christ, it applies to how I interact with others and how much I demonstrate respect for those with whom I am working.

In my personal situation, our bandleader asks me on a regular basis my preference for the sound of his drums. Do I like the drums tuned one way or another? Many times, he will choose my preference. (I am humbled that he values my opinion.) It's one thing to be asked one's opinion in an area of non-expertise. It is another to push or insist that I know what I am talking about.

Is Performing Worship a Performance?

The issue of performance in worship has become a debated topic. Some say if our worship is a performance, whether it be playing an instrument, singing, running tech, or preaching, we are glorifying self and not God. Second Samuel 6 tells the story of David and his men returning the Ark of the Covenant to the City of David.

> *And David and all the house of Israel were celebrating before the Lord, with songs and lyres and harps and tambourines and castanets and cymbals* (v.5).

> *A mighty celebration was taking place, and it involved the entire house of Israel. Then "David danced before the Lord with all his might. And David was wearing a linen ephod. So David and all the house of Israel brought up the ark of the Lord with shouting and with the sound of the horn* (vv.14-15).

It is difficult not to view this event as a grand performance of worship before the Lord. David danced with abandon. His joyous expression was with "all his might." It does not sound as if the musicians and especially David were restraining themselves. They fully engaged in an expression of worship that was pleasing to God. But there's a snare. David's wife Michal was offended with what she viewed as David's outlandish display.

> *When Michal the daughter of Saul came out to meet David she said, "How the king of Israel honored himself today, uncovering himself today before the eyes of his servants' female servants, as one of the vulgar fellows shamelessly uncovers himself!" And David said to Michal, "It was before the Lord, who chose me above your father and above all his house, to appoint me as prince over Israel, the people of the Lord—and I will celebrate before the Lord. I will make myself yet more contemptible than this, and I will be abased in your eyes. But by the female servants of whom you have spoken, by them I shall be held in honor." And Michal the daughter of Saul had no child to the day of her death.* (2 Samuel 6:20-23)

To the more casual reader, it may seem rather odd that God was pleased with David's worship, but that is not the point here. Rather, this example may help us understand some of the criteria of authentic worship. 1. It may or may not involve a visible performance. 2. What may seem as an excessive and unnecessary display of joy or emotion to some, may be perfectly acceptable before the Lord. 3. It is clear from the text that to judge another's authentic worship is not right in the eyes of God. Michal saw the dance as excessive, but she is rebuked and not David. 4. David did not perform his dance for the accolades of man but purely as an expression of joy before the Lord.

I am not suggesting that we engage in this type of worship publicly. We live in a vastly different age than that of King David. To see the Scripture in perspective, it is difficult if not impossible to remove the concept of performance from our services. Everyone is performing. The congregation is performing as they sing—some with noticeable motions, others without. The question arises, for whom are we performing?

Soren Kierkegaard answers the question directly. He says, "Worship isn't God's show. God is the audience. God's watching. The congregation, they are the actors in this drama. Worship is their show. And the minister is just reminding the people of their forgotten lines." We all have a responsibility to perform, sing, shout, repeat scripture, and be engaged in corporate worship. Worshipers—all involved in worship—should be taught and given the freedom to worship with a sense of abandon before the Lord, not in the least bit worried about what others think and only concerned with what God thinks.

Paul places boundaries in his instructions to the church at Corinth.

What then, brothers? When you come together, each one has a hymn, a lesson, a revelation, a tongue, or an interpretation. Let all things be done for building up. For God is not a God of confusion but of peace. But all things should be done decently and in order.
(1 Corinthians 14:26, 33, 40)

The principle of worshiping with abandon, while maintaining order and peace, plays heavily into the awareness of leaders, musicians, and techs as worship takes place. We should be aware of what is happening and recognize when something needs to be changed or stopped at the appropriate time.

Quality Vs. Perfection

Actor Peter O'Toole tells the story while on location in Saudi Arabia filming the movie *Lawrence of Arabia*: "Many years ago, I had a beloved leather jacket . . . and I never wanted to throw it away. I sent it to the cleaners because it was covered in blood and Guinness and Scotch and Corn Flakes, the usual. It went off to the Sycamore Cleaners and it came back with a thing pinned on it: 'It distresses us to return work which is not perfect'—so I want that on my tombstone."[5]

Our sinful nature causes great seduction. Easily peddled as virtue, it comes not from the object of our love, but rather from the one who is bent on our destruction. It is the driving desire to be perfect. Pride and her accomplice, perfection, parade as desirable, admirable qualities. When I nail the mix, a guitar lick, or complex drum pattern, I fall prey to the idea that perfection is possible.

For some of us, as it was for Peter O'Toole's cleaners, it distresses us to be less than perfect. At the same time, our perceived perfection triggers the rush of adrenaline. I want everyone to be thoroughly impressed with my ability to perform perfectly. When we are seduced by the pride of perfection, the enemy receives the glory.

When I was growing up, my father had an acute interest in film and media but especially sound. Dad had grown up with some of the Hollywood kids and was well acquainted with studios and film production. When we were small children living in Southern California, he would take us to the famous Warner Theatre in Hollywood to see Lowell Thomas' travel movies in Cinerama[6] or to see a religiously based movie such as Ben Hur. We were generally not allowed to see movies, but Dad made exceptions. One of the features of seeing large venue films at the Warner Theatre was intermission. During intermission, the keyboard for the mighty Wurlitzer pipe organ would rise out of the ground in a magnificent display of grandeur, and the organist would play mighty music on the enormous pipes of the theater.

Dad loved the sound of the Wurlitzer and told me if he could own his own, if he had the finances and a place to put it, he would. In a heartbeat, he would. As much as he desired a Wurlitzer pipe organ in our living room, he was not able. He was a science teacher, without a degree, living on a paltry salary.

When one of my aunts died, she left my dad a good sum of money. It was not enough to buy a Wurlitzer and remodel our home to house the mighty pipes, but it was enough to get us out of debt. Instead of paying bills, though, Dad decided to purchase a stereo system. Since my aunt taught music at a grammar school, Dad convinced us that the best way to honor her memory was to buy the best stereo system money could buy. And that he did. He purchased a complete, hi-end stereo system:

amplifier, preamp, and tuner.

In those days, the equipment was expensive (similar models are no less expensive today). When Dad set up the stereo, word spread fast, and people came from all over town to hear the amazing sound and quality. We were famous for a bit. We had one of the best systems in town.

Growing up with a high-end sound system at home while being exposed to the absolute best quality Hollywood had to offer taught me a lot about music and sound engineering. The bar was set extremely high at a noticeably young age. I could tell the difference between the popular, inexpensive sound systems and those systems that faithfully reproduced music. I learned how to listen for nuance and to appreciate performance. I believe his decision to introduce me to high-end audio is the reason I am still in high-end and professional audio today.

While I know how a sound system should sound, I am plagued with the desire to have the best, the highest quality. I am distressed that I cannot hear detailed nuance in the acoustic guitar, the beautifully articulated low notes of the piano, and right now, the drummer sounds as if he is kicking cardboard. To achieve the sound image that is in my head is difficult and expensive to achieve. The frustration and tension are real.

When we desire to provide the best sounding audio or musical instruments, a tension develops. What constitutes best sound? Is the best sounding necessary? Is it worth the cost? Does it make a difference? How can one decide? Am I worshiping the technology in my decisions, or am I worshiping the Creator of the universe, my Savior and Lord, and am I allowing Him to guide my decisions?

Given the task of building or improving a sound system, too often in our high-tech, ego- boosting, gadget-driven world, we rush to pick speakers and amplifiers and instruments first. We are bombarded with ads in worship magazines and blogs about the latest digital mixing console, smart amplifiers, or high-performance speakers. Pages are filled with the latest patches that emulate exactly a favored guitar, instrument, or effect. This stuff is cool. It appeals to the mojo.

Nothing is wrong with any of it or the use of it, but if we start only thinking first and foremost about the electronics and the gadgets and focus only on the best, we miss a fundamental question that must be asked. Do we need it? How will it enhance or improve the worship experience, if at all?

How often have these thoughts pervaded your mind: If I only had this microphone, I wouldn't strain my voice when singing; with this effects box, I can make my guitar sound just like *(fill in the blank)*; or with new speakers and amplifiers, we can achieve 120 decibels mid-house. When we focus on tech to solve perceived problems, we are putting the cart before the horse. Please don't misunderstand. There is a marked, noticeable difference between a $100 bargain guitar and a $1500 Martin. No comparison. Yet how does one decide?

A telling illustration is found in the story of Moses and the building of the tabernacle. In Exodus, we are told that Moses had been in unhindered, soul-changing singular worship of the Lord. When he descended from Mount Sinai (for a second time), he was carrying the Ten Commandments. His closeness to the Lord in worship was evidenced by his appearance to the children of Israel.

When Moses came down from Mount Sinai, with the two tablets

of the testimony in his hand as he came down from the mountain, Moses did not know that the skin of his face shone because he had talked with the Lord. (Exodus 34:29)

Then Moses gave Israel instructions regarding the construction of the tabernacle, the movable dwelling place of God intended to reside amid the Israelites. He calls to all of Israel for the materials to build the tabernacle. He calls to the Israelites to be generous and to bring the finest materials for the construction of the tabernacle.

Moses said to all the congregation of the people of Israel,

> *This is the thing that the Lord has commanded. Take from among you a contribution to the Lord. Whoever is of a generous heart, let him bring the Lord's contribution: gold, silver, and bronze; blue and purple and scarlet yarns and fine twined linen; goats' hair, tanned rams' skins, and goatskins; acacia wood, oil for the light, spices for the anointing oil and for the fragrant incense, and onyx stones and stones for setting, for the ephod and for the breastpiece.* (Exodus 35:4-9)

And then Moses calls for the laborers. He calls those by name whom God has given skill, ability, and talent; and he calls each one to use their talents for the glory of God.

> *Let every skillful craftsman among you come and make all that the Lord has commanded.*[7]

Then Moses said to the people of Israel,

> *See, the Lord has called by name Bezalel the son of Uri, son of Hur, of the tribe of Judah; and he has filled him with the Spirit of God, with skill, with intelligence, with knowledge, and with all craftsmanship, to devise artistic designs, to work in gold and silver and bronze, in cutting stones for setting, and in carving wood, for work in every skilled craft. And he has inspired him to teach, both him and Oholiab the son of Ahisamach of the tribe of Dan. He has filled them with skill to do every sort of work [emphasis author's] done by an engraver or by a designer or by an embroiderer in blue and purple and scarlet yarns and fine twined linen, or by a weaver—by any sort of workman or skilled designer.* (Exodus 35:30-35)

Our culture tends to appreciate gifts, talents, and abilities as given mostly to those in leadership, or at least to those who push an awareness of themselves. In the Bible, that is clearly not the case. Moses tells us that the Lord filled the workers and laborers with skill to do every sort of work. God called these men to do the work and gave them the skill to do so with excellence. The text goes on to explain how the finest materials and the most skilled laborers came together to construct a gloriously beautiful tabernacle. No expense was spared. The amount offered was more than needed—fifteen pounds of gold, silver, and bronze. The material and work were the highest quality just as the Lord had commanded. "And Moses saw all the work, and behold, they had done it; as the Lord had commanded, so had they done it. Then Moses blessed them."[8]

It was an honorable, magnificent calling to be a laborer with honed skill and ability to craft the seamless curtains, the ark, the elements of the holy place. All the skilled labor and work and all the extreme attention to detail were not the object of worship. The work was honoring of the One who called them, and He is the one who received the glory. It should be noted that there was no ceremony, no commemorative plaques, no engineering awards, and no banquet honoring and exalting the workers. Some key workers are given mention, while most are anonymous.

God's calling today is of no less importance with no less of attention to fine material and skilled labor. He calls for us to bring forward our best skills, abilities, and talents when serving Him. Each of us, who are members of the body of Christ, have been gifted with spiritual gifts, talents, and abilities to perform His work. We are to perform with excellence. We are to give our absolute best, with no excuses for shoddy workmanship or lackluster effort.

However, in our desire to provide the best of our ability (and we should not shrink from this responsibility), the temptation emerges for our labor and the product of our labors to be the objects of our worship. We may be able to build beautiful meeting places, design and install state-of-the-art sound systems with heart-pounding sound levels, and play music in a service that leaves the congregants speechless. If God is not honored first and foremost, though, all is for nothing. When we glorify our work rather than the One we serve, we are focusing sinfully on ourselves. Paul emphasizes this concept when he says,

> *For by the grace given to me I say to everyone among you not to think of himself more highly than he ought to think, but to think with sober judgment, each according to the measure of faith that God has assigned.*
> (Romans 12:3)

Rod Dreher talks of the first Benedictine monks and their disciplined daily lives.[9] They lived strict schedules built around prayer, worship, and labor. According to Dreher, Benedictine monks saw the life of a monk as whole, not compartmentalized. Eating, sleeping, working, resting, and praying was worship. Each part of life was informed by all other parts, and all worked together in harmony.

When it came to a monk's labor, the friars were careful, though, to closely observe the monks as they labored. For example, if a monk who worked in the wood shop making furniture and cabinets became too focused on the craft in order to achieve a greater quality, striving for perfection, they were removed for a period of time or reassigned so that the striving for perfection would not become a stumbling block. The friars did not want anything to come between a monk and authentic worship. The monks were taught to seek quality, not perfection.

I am not advocating for a denial or even suppression of God-given creativity and talent. Just the opposite. We are commanded to use our talents for His glory. What I am suggesting is within times of congregational worship, we temper our desire to create new or to stand out. The reason is spiritual, not artistic. Authentic worship requires intentional artistic constraint in order to allow all the congregation to participate in worship without the expectation of entertainment.

As an artist, I have individual God-given creative skills and talents. The expression of creativity in worship must come under a subjection to the greater good. That good is what invites, encourages, and amplifies the worship of the whole, and not of a single individual or group of individuals or any artistic expression.

In that regard, not congratulating each other on a worship performance makes sense. Perhaps we should train ourselves to be wholly satisfied with a simple thank you instead of accolades.

Are We Worshiping When We Are Performing Duties in Worship?

In some ways, the question is not a particularly good one. The issue never comes up in Scripture. For instance, Paul never states that the only time he was worshiping was when he was doing "spiritual" work. In other words, he does not compartmentalize life into spiritual and secular as if God was only pleased with Paul when he was doing the things that we have come to label in modern Christianity as spiritual. For Paul, sailing to get to a destination to preach was just as spiritual as preaching the Word when he arrived. No divisions. No compartmentalization.

I have asked the question, "Are we worshiping when we are performing duties in worship?" of pastors, musicians, and engineers, and have generally heard the following answers: 1. No. If the musician or tech is thinking about what they are doing, they are not worshiping. 2. Yes and No. When the musician or tech is not thinking about the next note or button, then they are worshiping. 3. Yes. We worship all the time in all that we do (if we are not sinning).

Francis Schaeffer Jr. says that when Jesus called Matthew to be an apostle and then called Nicodemus to the faith, he made no value judgment on which calling was greater. Matthew was called to the office and gifted as an apostle, a leader in the church. Nicodemus was called to be honest, to not overcharge, and to treat all men fairly. Both were called. Both callings were spiritual, and both worshiped as they worked out their own salvation and individual calling. Jesus did not favor one over the other.[10] In the same manner, we each have been called, given gifts and talents to be used for the kingdom of God. In the context of sound for worship, each is worshiping as we exercise our gifts and talents before the Lord. Pushing a button, playing a note, or even thinking about singing the next note is not unspiritual.

As noted earlier, I was in charge of sound for a medium-sized church where the sound booth was, according to the architect, appropriately placed on a second story behind a glass window. The idea was that the FOH should be out of sight and out of mind. The first thing I did was to stop the installation of the glass window. I wanted to have a sense of the sound in the auditorium and wanted to hear as much of what was happening as I could.

I will never forget the struggles I went through to understand the mix from the perspective of a second-floor booth. It took over two years to calibrate my brain to the sound I heard in the booth (and the booth support speakers) and how it correlated to the sound on the floor. I also felt that during that time, I did not enter worship. I was too focused on the mechanics of sound to think about worship and being part. Once I achieved "muscle memory" and could free my mind to think more about worship, then I felt I able to take part.

In retrospect, my perspective was wrong. I was worshiping the entire time. As I listened, mixed, and labored over the sound, God was being served and honored. I was performing worship with my God-given talents and skills.

Harold Best puts it this way, David calls us "to sing 'to the Lord.' These three simple words . . . make it clear that singing is above all an act of worship, an offering to the Lord and not to people . . . Performers should understand that their performance is directed to God while people listen in, not the opposite."[11]

Questions: Do you have the proper perspective on professionalism, quality, and performance? Do you seek attention for your role, or do you perform your role out of the heart of a grateful, loving servant? Have you been tempted or acted upon the temptation for "me first" (e.g. I must increase and everyone else must decrease.)

Chapter 5

Chaos, Tension, and Collateral Damage

"And the Lord's servant must not be quarrelsome but kind to everyone, able to teach, patiently enduring evil, correcting his opponents with gentleness" (2 Timothy 2:24-25).

"There is quiet confidence in knowing we all hit a couple of wrong notes here and there. The report card on our faith is how we treat one another when they do" (Bob Goff, Instagram).

"Love difficult people. You're one of them" (Bob Goff).

"You don't have a good story without tension and conflict, without things going wrong" (Paul Miller, A Praying Life).

Busy By Nature

We live in a culture that places a high value on busyness. Busyness—being a workaholic—is a core societal value. It is worshiped as a sign of success. Some are truly busy, while others give off the appearance of being busy. Whatever a person's situation is, work life, home/family life, and church life must be woven together. Each area of our life requires attention. While we desire a seamless weaving of all the elements of life, to be truthful, the weave is rough and not just around the edges. Tension can erupt as each area of life conflicts with the other—in time spent, prioritization, and demands placed upon us. Sometimes, as church volunteers, we are fitting in our service to the body of Christ where we are able.

When we serve in the church, sometimes we come with the stuff of all the other areas of life hanging to us and at times dragging behind us. We may try to hide or disguise our baggage, but it's there. It's baggage from our childhood, from school, from growing up, from our family, from previous jobs, from current jobs, from all parts of our life. It announces its presence at the most inopportune times. The tense conversation with my boss at work today becomes the hidden reason that I am sullen and upset. The argument I had with my wife over the finances has not yet been resolved, and I am carrying a chip on my shoulder, insisting I am right.

Whatever the circumstances are, and everyone has circumstances, these spill into rehearsals, conversations, interactions, and into the time of worship. What we do with our baggage in those moments and the tensions that may ensue is what defines us as either willing, joyful servants, or grousing, kick-the-can (or the dog) complainers.

Tension[1] in Music

"In music, tension is the anticipation music creates in a listener's mind for relaxation or release. For example, tension may be produced through reiteration, increase in dynamic level, gradual motion to a higher or lower pitch, or (partial) syncopations between consonance and dissonance."[2]

Tension is necessary for stringed instruments to play. Applying various levels of tension to an instrument's strings produces a different range of notes. The vocal cords are brought into a state of tension to produce sounds and sing notes. Lips are pursed in tension to produce the sounds of a horned instrument. Without tension, music is not formed.

The art of music is all about tension and release. Creating moments of unrest and building an instrumental turmoil requires a subsequent resolution. This progression of tension and release hooks listeners as they begin to feel that moment of liberation at the end. When done right, this musical "conflict" is subtle, yet moving, and keeps listeners coming back for more. There are several different ways to achieve this when you are writing and playing music, and all are important to consider during the creative process.[3]

If the music can be "in tension and conflict," we humans may be in even greater conflict, and as Franky Schaeffer says, we engage in "clashing harmony." Evangelical worship wars have generated more tension, more conflict, and more dissonance and clashing harmony than any doctrinal issue faced by the modern church. Much of our tension results in continued dissonance without achieving a harmonic rest. We fight, we grouse, we want our way or the highway—harmony and unity be damned.

Stuff Happens, Always Does

It was the morning of a special day in the life of a church. A minister was being formally acknowledged in a church event highlighting his ordination. The auditorium was packed with family, friends, members of the church, and a large number of ordained pastors who were there to give support and give charge to the minister, the congregation, and for the prayer of ordination.

At first arrival I was cornered by a band member. "Pray, pray, pray. The rehearsal went terrible." When I greeted the FOH for the morning, he did not look happy and said, "Many, many problems this morning." I prayed. When the first song was sung, I was wondering about the meaning of the concern. The music sounded good, strong, and with full congregational singing. The second congregational song was even more powerful. I continued to wonder where the problems were. Then stuff happened. At the welcome, the MC's hand-held wireless microphone started cutting in and out. This microphone had been a flawless performer for years.

I asked myself, *Why is this happening now, today of all days?* I left my seat and hurried to the booth. The engineer gave me another wireless mic, and I rushed to the front to hand the MC the replacement microphone. While we exchanged microphones, the MC said, "So will this one work?" I nodded and said yes under my breath while quickly moving off stage. But as soon as the FOH opened the microphone, a high-pitched squeal filled the room, not once but twice. Finally, the sound settled, and we moved on. I found myself hoping this issue would be the only problem. It wasn't.

Two pastors from other churches were giving the charge to the newly ordained pastor and one to the congregation. When the first pastor stepped to the podium to give his charge, his headset mic cut in and out. *Here we go again,* I thought. The FOH rushed to where I was sitting and handed me another hand-held wireless mic. I quickly moved to the stage in the middle of the charge and apologized while giving the mic to the pastor. He said, "So I don't need this thing!" as he tore off his wireless headset and threw it over his shoulder. The audience laughed. I felt about the size of a pea right then and was annoyed and humiliated.

One of the frustrations for me that day was that the sound and media team had worked hard to be professional and consistent over the years, with a minimum of distractions and mess-ups during the worship services. The simple fact is stuff happens. In unpredictable ways. The question is, what is our response considering the tension and failures? Is what I have described really a failure?

Sometimes conflicts arise over talent and style. I have worked with musicians who during practice play the notes and chords perfectly, but during the worship service somehow miss the notes or a chord entirely. I have also worked with FOHs who miss when to unmute a vocalist's microphone. The vocalist starts to sing, but little to nothing is heard. I have seen this scenario all too often, when someone steps up to the podium to speak and pushes the microphone away, proclaiming they don't need a microphone.

All these actions cause tension and may disrupt the service. The worship service can become dissonant, lacking harmony, and become difficult to continue without being distracted. If left uncorrected, the distraction may go on for a while. Fallout among the musicians and sound team can cause further tension, hurt feelings, and lack of unity and harmony in the team.

Tensions and Chaos Without Sin

In contrast to the ordination service, my wife told me of a concert she attended recently. The singer is a nationally known artist and commands a large audience. My wife told me that during one portion of the event, the singer's wireless handheld microphone stopped working, but the singer kept talking, only louder, not losing a beat, setting the microphone aside. The crew took a bit to get her another microphone that worked.

According to my wife, the singer never once made a derogatory remark and never once criticized the sound team. When the microphone failed, she simply kept talking. She knew the priorities and kept her opinions, whatever those may have been, to herself.

Much patience is required to weather technical failures when singing or preaching. I have preached at our church on occasions when nothing seemed to be on cue technically. Problems like these are off-putting and frustrating when they occur. They may be as a result of a mistake, or they may be something out of our control (like a fully-charged microphone stops working). Our attitudes, demeanor, and language at a time when things are not working says a lot about our priorities. Too often, our responses fall flat, and the enemy advances his kingdom.

I am most intrigued by the response of the singer my wife described. Her humility, patience, and trust in the Lord overarched the situation. The singer allowed the event to continue, unhindered by any comments that would have distracted from the primary purpose of the concert—to give glory to God and not to herself.

Another wonderful and challenging example of tension and chaos without sin comes from a music pastor and teacher. I first met Levi[4] during a lecture I was conducting on the topic of Sound for Worship. Levi is first and foremost a pastor— a seminary trained and ordained pastor. He is also an accomplished musician, songwriter, and teacher of the Word. As pastor, he takes the mandate seriously to shepherd the hearts and minds of the people: to keep the unity, protect against heresy, and guard the flock. Levi has a deep love for Christ and for the church.

In the lecture, I discuss what to do if a musician or singer is consistently off-key or lacks rhythm and timing. Levi was in the class and told the story of working with a singer who sings off-key and lacks timing. This person plays the piano as well but lacks the understanding of current musical style. As he leads singing, Levi says he is at times thrown off by this person's lack of musical skill. Contrary to conventional wisdom, Levi has not removed the person from the music team even though he has professional conservatory-trained musicians on the team.

As Levi told his story, an immediate response came from others in the class. Some suggested he was soft or lacking in leadership if he did not remove the person from the team. To most, it was obvious. Either you are a good musician, or you are not in the band. Period. But Levi took exception to the conventional wisdom. The mediocre singer/piano player was welcome on the team because of his or her demonstrated godliness. This person would not normally qualify to be in the band, but had, during a bout with a serious illness, glorified God. The person worshiped Him, trusted Him, and demonstrated a rare humility. Levi said that though there was no conscientious, intelligent conclusion one could draw to leave the person on the team, the person's humility (I must decrease, He must increase) kept the individual on the team.

When pressed again on the decision, Levi said the choice was not a musical decision but a spiritual one. The decision is about what is best for the congregation and what is best for worship.

Levi's manner of leading includes conducting a devotional before rehearsal each week to guide the musicians to hunger and thirst for the Lord first and foremost. He sees the team as worshipers first, musicians second.

How we respond to events that lead to tension says a great deal about our view of worship. Authentic worship, and the practice thereof (as addressed in Chapter 3), is the starting point for understanding how to respond and manage continuing human tension and dissonance. Timothy warns against being at odds with each other. He says, "And the Lord's servant must not be quarrelsome but kind to everyone, able to teach, patiently enduring evil, correcting his opponents with gentleness" (2 Timothy 2:24-25).

While we may be taught to recognize the attacks of enemy, we rarely are taught or expect "friendly fire." Levi has experienced much friendly fire from his own congregation for his choice to leave a less-than-talented musician in the band. If our focus is anything other than authentic worship, we will be ill-prepared for handling the kind of attacks that come from within the body of Christ and those in the body with whom we work on a day-to-day basis. First and foremost, our response must be routed in Scripture. To paraphrase 1 Corinthians 13:1-3 in the context of sound for worship, "If I achieve an awesome band, the best sound, high quality singing, but I don't have love, all is for nothing and useless."

Consider Romans 12:3 where Paul warns that we are not to think too highly of ourselves and put others before our own interests.[5] In a performance-based culture where expectations for worldly performance are applied to the worship services, approaching tensions calmly and in love is indeed challenging. Some may see the issue as, "If I don't fix the problem, I will be viewed as unprofessional or sloppy. I may even be out of a job."

Sometimes, and this is counterintuitive, the obvious tension or problem may not be resolved immediately in favor of something greater. Levi looked for the greater. When I first heard Levi's story, I immediately disagreed with him. The more he explained, however, the more I was convinced that his love for the person and his love of Christ was working in a manner that Christ was glorified through his decision. Rather than immediately remove a person who is not the best at what they do (sometimes there is no other choice), is it possible to see the circumstance in light of Scripture? Aren't we all unique members of the body of Christ? Being unique members, each of us has a place of service—it may just take some time to get good at the acts of service we are being asked to do.

The more difficult decision in Levi's case would come if the singer, singing off-key, was disruptive to the service and to the natural flow of the service. If the singer's microphone could not be managed so that the singer was not dominate in the mix, then a tougher decision might be in order.

Honor Each Other

Several years ago, a popular singer/composer was scheduled to lead the singing during our morning worship service. At the time, I was teaching an adult Bible class the hour before service and would rush to the sound booth after class to run sound for worship. The singer was not at the early morning setup or rehearsal, and I (mistakenly) was not concerned. He was a professional and only needed a microphone at the piano, or so I was told.

At about halfway through my hour-long class, the music

minister was at my door and out of breath. I was needed immediately. The guest singer had a complicated set of songs and needed special setup. By the time I was able to meet the guest, we had less than ten minutes to review a complex setup. Sitting on my console was a large stack of tapes that needed to accompany the singer while he played the piano. Some of the tapes required pitch shifting. Others needed tight cueing. To add more difficulty, the singer told me that he may skip some songs and would give me a signal to let me know when to skip. (This caused a great deal of anxiety on my part during the service as I second-guessed whether he had truly given the signal or not.)

The guest singer also told me that the tight cue on some songs had to be precise. The tape had to start precisely at the moment he hit the first note on the piano. We did all the prep (without rehearsal) in less than ten minutes. And then he said something I will never forget. He told me, if I honored him in the performance, he would honor me. Though much perspiration flowed (I was a young FOH at the time), the performance was flawless. The singer was true to his promise, and he honored me and thanked me for my work in front of the congregation.

Bestowing honor is seen in Paul and his dealings with John Mark, but it didn't start off in an honorable fashion. And after some days Paul said to Barnabas, "Let us return and visit the brothers in every city where we proclaimed the word of the Lord, and see how they are." Now Barnabas wanted to take with them John called Mark. But Paul thought best not to take with them one who had withdrawn from them in Pamphylia and had not gone with them to the work. And there arose a sharp disagreement, so that they separated from each other. Barnabas took Mark with him and sailed away to Cyprus, but Paul chose Silas and departed, having been commended by the brothers to the grace of the Lord. And he went through Syria and Cilicia, strengthening the churches (Acts 15:36-41).

At this point in Paul's ministry, he did not want John Mark on his team. Mark was not valuable to Paul because Mark had abandoned the ministry at a time when he was needed most. By the end of Paul's life, though, while in prison, Paul sent for Mark.

> *Luke alone is with me. Get Mark and bring him with you, for he is very useful to me for ministry.* (1 Timothy 4:11)

For me, this is a heartwarming portion of Scripture. In Paul's final days on earth, he wanted the company and help of Mark in ministry. Honor bestowed. Conflict and tension resolved.

From a godly perspective, all disciples are useful in the kingdom of God and required of God to serve and move the kingdom forward. In the local church, all are not only useful, but required, if we are to build the kingdom of God.

Seek Joy

> *But now I am coming to you, and these things I speak in the world, that they may have my joy fulfilled in themselves.* (John 17:13)

Can we find the joy of the Lord during chaos? When all is crashing down around us, when nothing seems to be working properly in our worship service, can we experience the peace and joy that only comes from authentic worship? Jesus said that the joy we can have is *His* joy, not our own. What's the difference?

In the case of the ordination service described earlier, the microphone problems were taken in stride by the local staff with the understanding that we are not perfect, and technology is not perfect. The bandleader said it best while giving me a huge smile. "It wasn't just you. The band had problems as well. Despite our mess-ups, God was here, and He was honored. We can screw stuff up, but He makes it all work together for good, for His glory." In the end, joy was sought. I have experienced exactly the opposite response all too many times.

In the next chapter, I address further how to achieve harmony by understanding how the gifts of the Holy Spirit impact our worship services.

Questions: Have you experienced tension among the band members, crew, or staff? Have you viewed the tension (or chaos) as an opportunity to seek unity, or have you viewed it as an annoyance? What can you do to reduce personality tension and seek the joy that should be in every worship service? What are some demonstrative actions you personally can take to reduce tension between the band and the sound team?

Chapter 6

No Man Is an Island

(A Biblical Perspective on Serving Worship)

"For by the grace given to me I say to everyone among you not to think of himself more highly than he ought to think, but to think with sober judgment, each according to the measure of faith that God has assigned" (Romans 12:3).

"Even the Son of Man came not to be served but to serve, and to give his life as a ransom for many" (Mark 10:45).

The Heart of a Servant

"No man is an island entire of itself; every man is a piece of the continent, a part of the main; if a clod be washed away by the sea, Europe is the less, as well as if a promontory were, as well as any manner of thy friends or of thine own were; any man's death diminishes me, because I am involved in mankind. And therefore, never send to know for whom the bell tolls; it tolls for thee."[1]

There is an unexpectable joy and peace ("not as the world gives") when wholly and completely serving the Lord with the gifts and talents He has given to us by His grace. The joy of service (beyond human description) is manifold. The expectation and realization of joy confirms within us that we have been "called according to his purposes" (Romans 8:28).

Our giftedness, though, is not our own. We have not earned, nor have we determined, our gifts. We have not willed them to fruition through hard labor and sacrifice. They have been birthed and nourished in us solely and completely by His determinative will. We are commanded to use the gifts He has given us. When we apply our gifts in the works of the kingdom, we fulfill our calling to perform good works.

The blunt reality is that serving in the body, no matter the place of service or the church, can be a messy business and is not for the faint of heart. Though we are commanded to be servants, it is a challenge not to be discouraged, frustrated, or burned out from criticism that is anything but constructive. Scripture offers no wiggle room for us to live as Simon and Garfunkel suggest in one of their songs—as an island rock. We are not to isolate ourselves. Instead, we are to be open and vulnerable. Knowing I am to be this kind of servant does not make it any easier, though.

I can't tell you the number of times I have been told how to do my job and what to do by people that have nothing to do with or any knowledge of what the job is. An incredible amount of grace is necessary not to act snarky or talk back or talk down. Some can be infinitely patient and gracious. Others are not. Even if the person doing the telling is well versed in what needs to take place, the interactions and responses are often less than stellar.

Several principles are at work when we feel the need to correct another person or tell them what to do. First and foremost, most church attenders do not have a clear understanding of the nature of the body of Christ and service within the body. As noted before, worldly principles tend to be followed in the church today rather than sound biblical principles. Dennis Dirks, Emeritus Dean of Talbot Seminary, has asked me time and time again, "Are you willing to be unknown for your work?"

The biblical narrative on gifts of the Holy Spirit provide clear guidance on gifts and the exercise of gifts and talents within the body of Christ. First Peter 4:10 says, "As each has received a gift, use it to serve one another, as good stewards of God's varied grace." In 1 Corinthians 12, Paul explains that all members of the body have different gifts, but all come from the same Spirit.

Jesus taught with clarity when He instructed the disciples on their attitude toward serving. Jesus said, "even the Son of Man came not to be served but to serve, and to give his life as a ransom for many" (Mark 10:45).

Paul brings further clarity in that we all serve together.

> *For just as each of us has one body with many members, and these members do not all have the same function, so in Christ we, though many, form one body, and each member belongs to all the others. We have different gifts, according to the grace given to each of us.*
> (Romans 12:4-6 NIV)

Finding a Servant

After years of ministry as pastor, professor, seminary dean, (and brother) Dennis Dirks believes we must take a more rigorous approach when seeking and placing people in ministry positions in the body. Many times, we appoint a person to a position of ministry simply because they have leadership responsibilities or skills in their secular job that would apply. For instance, a church may be extremely excited to have a professional piano player in the church. Leadership may feel that person could greatly enhance the worship services and bring a greater sense of quality and professionalism to the entire worship team.

Dennis suggests that these skills and abilities may or may not apply or be appropriate for use in the body. First and foremost, is the person a true disciple of Jesus Christ? If we place nonbelievers in musical leadership positions, we cause damage to the effective work of the Holy Spirit.

Any person being considered for leadership or a position with the worship team must be prayerfully considered and personally interviewed. Dennis states that it is not enough to be a Christian, the person's heart must be right before the Lord. It's a character issue. He offers some interview questions that could be used prior to placement of a person in leadership.[2]

Ask questions that probe the condition of the person's heart. Do they understand biblical commands regarding worship? Are they living and particularly serving based on those commands in their role in worship? Do they genuinely love others and demonstrate that love?

1. *Whose kingdom do we serve?* While this may seem obvious, many times the kingdom being served is of the earth and not of heaven. Often it is a personal kingdom.

2. *What are your idols?* How would you respond to a comment that whatever your role on the worship team is your idol?" Asking these questions may take some time and patience. We all have idols, those areas of our life that we have trouble bringing into subjection of the Holy Spirit. Possible idols may be music or playing music. A sound engineer may love sound or technology more than God. The idea is not to judge, but to find people who will worship the Creator rather than the creation.

3. What is your biblical theological understanding of the purpose of the position you are filling?

4. Are you teachable; are you willing to be trained? What would demonstrate that you are teachable? Get as specific as possible.

5. When trained, are you willing to share your knowledge and training with others? How would you mentor or train others?

6. How do you respect other members of the body and their gifts? (per 1 Corinthians 12).

7. Can you handle being unknown or not thanked by others for your work? How would you wrestle with being unknown? What attitudes and emotions come forward as you think about this?

8. What is your first thought when criticized? What is first feeling? How do you handle it?

Another possible question, "How you feel when things go wrong?" "When something goes wrong, how do you react?" Give examples..

Some of these questions may seem complicated or too in-depth for most Christians. The tendency would be to shy away from asking anything that would make the person being interviewed uncomfortable. There may also be a tendency to approach this process with a certain attitude that can be off-putting to others who are seeking to serve. The intent is to be just the opposite. We serve together. We grow in our faith and knowledge together. No one is superior.

Some of these questions may not be answered or may not be answered well. I encourage you to see the questions as a process rather than using it to achieve a checked-off questionnaire (and a good grade). Use these sets of questions as opportunities to teach, instruct, and guide each volunteer in a biblical understanding of the role of a servant in the body of Christ.

Encouragement First

You can focus on talent, skill, abilities, technology, or on people. You will be taken in vastly different paths depending on which path you chose. Throughout my career I have operated on a bit of a hybrid that is sometimes tech first, people second. Recently I have seen the problems a tech-approach can produce and have significantly shifted my emphasis to people and their success rather than simply being the best tech. Perfection in tech can be your enemy.There is no wiggle room when we study the Scriptures. If the Creator of the universe did not demand that He be served, how can we demand others serve us?

While the challenges to serving in the body are manifold, the grace of our Lord Jesus Christ is greater. There exists for the taking the unlimited flow of joy that comes from serving the body and knowing that our Lord is saying, "Well done."

Questions: How can you personally help to break the cycle of simply using a warm body or a talented person to fill a role that is needed within the band or media team? Does the process outlined seem too complicated and too lengthy to accomplish? Or is it doable to achieve the goal of seeking the person God has selected for the role.

PART III

Taming the Beast

(Applying Sound Theology to Sound Technology)

"The shop, the barn, the scullery, and the smithy, become temples when men and women do all to the glory of God" (Charles Spurgeon).

Chapter 7

More than Gear and Gearheads

"The truth is, most of us discover where we are heading when we arrive" (Bill Watterson, Calvin and Hobbs).

Sound Perception

Sound perception is a very personal. We all have ideas and preferences for the way the world around us sounds and the way it should sound. Our perception is not delusional. It is reality.[1] The brain is wired to respond to our highly individual perceptions. When we listen to music, for example, we may favor certain instruments or certain voices. In our mind, those elements are the most important, as if those instruments or voices are dominant in the performance.

Many people have a definite and pronounced preference for hearing clearly (and sometimes loudly) the bass line of a song. With that preference, mid-range sounds are ignored. High frequencies may not matter. This manner of listening, though popular, is a highly individualistic preference and perception.

Sound preference phenomenon can be applied to the

experience that happens when I listen to a song over and over. For any number of times, I may hear the song a certain way with vocals and instruments weaved together in a pleasing fashion. I may then conclude what I hear is the way the song was recorded or performed.

Then on some occasion, for no particular reason (other than maybe my allergies are not attacking, or I got a really good night's rest) I hear an instrument in the mix that intrigues me. The normal reaction to this event would be to ask or wonder, *What changed? Why am I hearing the music this way now? I have never heard the song like this before.* The reality may be nothing has changed. My brain has just noticed something it had not heard prior. In other words, we hear what we want to hear. (Please don't mention this to my wife.)

The brain also has certain reference points for the way a sound is perceived. It has an amazing ability to distinguish live sound from recorded sound. A friend of mine and I were discussing this recently. He talked of the experience of walking on the sidewalk in front of a club playing a live jazz band. In this situation, there may be loud street noise, doors and walls in between him and the band, and other less-than-ideal acoustical issues. Even with all the interference and competing noises, my friend says that he can tell that the band and the sax solo are live, not recorded. The brain can process sound that precisely.

When planning the sounds of worship, taking personal preference and propensities into account is important.

Everyone has preference and preconceived ideas about how sound should sound. Very few will agree. Moreover, strong personalities with strong opinions can and do intimidate others into thinking what they hear is correct, pushing others in disagreement to believe they are wrong. The power of suggestion is indeed powerful.

For instance, musicians and sound engineers disagree a great deal on what constitutes "correct" sounds. We argue as if there really is a correct sound! As you work through the process of understanding how to build the sounds of worship, you must be aware of the personal propensities for sound in yourself, the musicians, the technical team, and most importantly in the congregation.

Question: Are you willing to build a sound structure and atmosphere for worship while not insisting on your own perceptions?

What Is Sound Reinforcement?

Sound reinforcement is a system made up of amplifiers, speakers, mixers, microphones, and interconnection cable to provide the amplification of voices and musical instruments. Depending on the venue, some voices (strong ones) and instruments (horns and drums, etc.) may not need sound reinforcement in order to be heard. While other soft voices and instruments must have amplification (such as electro-pianos, synthesizers, etc.). In a setting for worship, sound reinforcement is often required to allow for a consistent mix of all voices and instruments during the service.

The Purpose of Sound Reinforcement

The purpose of sound reinforcement is "to provide undistorted, intelligible sound to the ears of the listeners [the congregation]. It is about hearing. If the sound is not intelligible, distorted, too loud, too soft, the listener will be distracted from the message."[2] The "message" in worship comes through words spoken and sung and not through music. The words must be heard clearly. The words must be intelligible.

When considering the need for sound reinforcement, the basic principle is not loudness or heart-thumping sound, it is about whether the listener can clearly hear the words being sung or spoken. Proper sound allows the congregant, without distraction, to enter into a congregational act of worship. During the singing, if the singers or band are too loud or distorted, congregational singing will be inhibited. If too soft, the congregation will miss the aural cues on what to sing next or what to do. If the preacher is too loud, older members may turn off their hearing aids. If too soft, they will strain to understand.

A key technical principle that is not difficult to understand is the principle of the articulation of consonants. "Human speech is interesting in that the vowels or voiced sounds from the vocal cords produce most of the sound power compared with the consonants. But consonants, while lower in energy, carry the necessary information needed to distinguish similar sounding words from each other. For speech to be intelligible, a listener needs to be able to clearly distinguish the different consonants sounds."[3] Intelligibility is affected by the system frequency response, the signal-to-noise ratio, and by the natural acoustics of the environment. (More on this in Chapter 9.) You can identify a sound system with poor articulation of consonants by a muffled sound with poorly articulated words.

When considering a sound system, the tendency is to start with what the musicians or the band needs or requires. The requirements may include the necessity of achieving a certain sound level that can only be achieved with a certain set of speakers, floor monitors, amplifiers, and microphones. This is the wrong starting point and ignores the reason for the time of worship in the first place. Always start with the listener, the person sitting in the congregation. Ask yourself, what *must* they hear? *How* will they hear it?

Demographics[4]

It is imperative as you work through the process to recognize that not all listeners "hear" in the same manner. Some may be loudness aversive, such as those mentioned with hearing aids. Dependent on the quality of the hearing aid, some may need some special attention.[5] Others are simply loud sound adverse and prefer a quiet service. Still others want to be knocked on the floor with heart-pounding sound. Is it possible to plan to accommodate any demographic that attends your church? Are you prepared to change how you deliver sound in order to meet the requirements of different demographics? If you are in a small-sized church, the size this book is written for (around 100 in attendance), then you most likely have a very wide and diverse congregation with many different requirements.

The challenges can be monumental. One pastor told me of a group of ex-convicts who were bused to his church every Sunday from a halfway house. After a few services, one of the ex-cons told the pastor that the group of them was having difficulty keeping up with the singing and with the message. The information was coming too fast and too loud for them to process.

Too many times when confronted with special needs in our services, we are quick to dismiss it or perhaps propose a Band-Aid fix, rather than addressing the need. I have heard leaders tell me that if a person complains about the sound being too loud, send them to the Cry Room where the sound is much more controlled. When it comes to ex-cons asking for the pastor to slow everything down and turn the volume down a bit, how would you respond?

Being Intentional

While it may seem idealistic, it is crucial for all people involved in worship services— pastors, music leads, musicians, sound and media techs—to discuss, understand, and intentionally plan for the kind of sound reinforcement that will be used. If no intentional thought and planning is in the process of establishing a sound system, the result will be less than desirable at best, and not functional at worst. At the forefront is the communication of

God's Word. Nothing should be allowed to stand in the way, especially the technology.

Questions: Do your preconceived concepts of sound interfere with your ability to work with others to develop appropriate sound for worship? Does knowing sound from a disciplined musical perspective trump others' knowledge of sound? Does knowing sound from a disciplined technical and acoustic perspective trump others' knowledge? How would you handle a demographic in your congregation (like the example of the ex-cons) to ensure they were able to enter congregational worship with everyone else?

Chapter 8

Built to Last:

Not Your Daddy's Boombox

"There will always be a desire for good sound and a general lack of understanding in attaining it. So not everybody will just be able to throw together a sound system with any sort of good or even mediocre results" (Jim Long, Electro-Voice).[1]

Bright Ideas

The new church building was nearly complete. The church was moving from a building that would hold only 100 people to one that hold nearly 500. All that remained was finishing the walls and laying the carpet. Then one astute person said, "What sound system should we use?" In the existing space, the church had purchased a standard, off-the-shelf mixer and column speaker system. The salesman had assured the church deacon board that this was the last sound system that they would ever need. Famous words!

For the new church building, a deacon who thought he understood the problem suggested that the church buy a set of stereo speakers, "the big kind," with a 1000-watt amplifier that would work perfectly, just like his home stereo. The deacon reassured the church board that putting in a sound system was not expensive and easy to do. Others suggested nothing at all to start with. After all, why is a sound system needed in the first place? The piano is loud enough. And people can just speak up.

At this point I stepped in. I had just completed training in sound system design at Syn- Aud-Con and had already spent ten years in the audio industry. I told the pastor and board that what was needed was a complete acoustic analysis followed by a sound system design. The pastor and the church board were dubious. To them, I was just another member of the congregation who was promoting an idea. They leaned strongly in the direction of two large stereo speakers.

Fight Conventional Wisdom

Richard Feynman was right. When speaking outside one's area of expertise, one can be just as dumb as the next person. When considering the design or upgrade of a sound reinforcement system, it is easy to fall prey to the conventional wisdom: "I have a great stereo at home I put together myself; therefore, I know how to build a sound system for the church." Or "My friend has a cousin who knows how to solder. He can put the system in for free." The reality is that home stereos and sound reinforcement systems have two totally different sets of requirements and functionality. While similarities exist, both have the function of amplifying sound; there is no functional equivalency. As Jim Long of Electro-Voice says, "Not everybody will just be able to throw together a sound system with any sort of good or even mediocre results."

Start at the Beginning - Always

Since we have defined the sound reinforcement system and the general goals for implementing it, let's turn our attention to some specifics. As noted in the beginning of the book, my goal is not to cover sound design in detail but to provide an overview of the important aspects in order to achieve a functioning sound system that meets its *intended* use. Beginning with the end in mind applies here. We need a clear vision of what we are building with the anticipated end results in mind.

Whether or not you have access to professional sound designers and acoustics experts, it's a good idea for you and the team to understand the environment (room) in which you are working. It is important to be able to have credible information to share with whomever performs the sound system design. I encourage you to take the time to go through this process. It will pay large dividends later.

Where to start? We like to start with the music and what technology is needed to amplify and communicate our songs. We want to talk about amps and mixing consoles and what kind of speakers we would install. But this is the wrong place to start. The starting point is with the listener, the person who sits in the chairs or pews of your worship space.

I encourage you to start by thinking about the listener and most importantly how they can more easily participate and perform in worship. The process is more effective if you do it with more than just yourself. Having the entire music and technical team participate would be greatly beneficial. Take notes. These notes will help you communicate what you need to a professional acoustical engineer and/or sound design engineer.

Acoustics

To begin with, the vast majority of church buildings, sanctuaries, and auditoriums are not designed for good sound or proper acoustics. Most churches use rooms that were never intended for singing and listening clearly to the spoken word. Acoustics is rarely taken into consideration.[2] This has not always been the case. The Mormon Tabernacle in Salt Lake City was built in the years 1864 to 1867 in an era prior to the invention of electronic sound amplification. The tabernacle seats 3700 people and has the reputation of being the most acoustically perfect building in the world. A person standing at the pulpit can be heard perfectly at every seat in the house, without microphone, amplifier, or speaker. The Mormon docents love to demonstrate this by dropping a pin/needle on the pulpit and watching as the visitors smile in amazement as they clearly hear the sound, no matter what part of the tabernacle in which they are sitting. The acoustic design of the tabernacle was intentional.

The early builders of the cathedrals understood sound

well. The lush, long reverberant sounds manifested in a cathedral perfectly magnify the instruments and voices raised in worship. Sitting in St. Stephen's Cathedral in Passau, Germany, is both reverential and awe-inspiring. The pipe organ is one of the largest in the world with almost 18,000 pipes ranging in size from 6 mm to 30 meters. At St. Stephen's, the acoustic delay amplifies the magnificent music written and arranged for the pipe organ. When the last note of Bach's "Jesu, Joy of Man's Desiring" is played, the reverberant delay sustains the note in a seemingly infinite state.

In this setting, I do not talk immediately. I do not rise quickly to get out of the sanctuary for lunch or rush to find a friend to talk sports with. I sit quietly, reverently, and ponder the awesome nature of our God.[3] I slow down, enjoy, and worship Him. The acoustic design was intentional.

At the Dolby Labs facility at 100 Potrero Avenue in San Francisco, Dolby engineers designed a 100-seat theater that can be acoustically tuned for any function taking place in the theater. Around the perimeter of the seating, concrete blocks and acoustic panels can be moved to "tune" the room. The area can be tuned to perfectly represent a THX DOLBY theater. It can be tuned for the natural amplification of the spoken voice. It can be tuned for an orchestra or band. The Dolby theater is one that I never tired of attending. The sound is natural and comfortable. When watching the first ten minutes of the movie *Fugitive* with Harrison Ford, the train wreck not only looks but feels real. I used to say that it felt as if the train were literally sitting in my lap. The acoustic design of the Dolby theater was intentional.

Every room is different. Every room has a different acoustical signature. Starting at the beginning of design with acoustics means that you, just like the examples here, are intentional about designing the environment for worship. As you look at the room and the requirements for sound, keep in mind the fact that it is easy to overreact and over-design for a room. Contemporary evangelical church music requires neither acoustically dead sound space nor the lavish long reverberant delays of a cathedral. A small amount of reverb in the one to two second range is helpful to naturally amplify voices and enhancing congregational singing.

Orthopraxy (Correct conduct or practice)

Start by making simple logical steps. Sit in the seat of a congregant and observe the environment (the church building)—the walls, the ceiling, the floors, and the placement of everything in the room. First and foremost, does the room provide an environment that is conducive to the worship of our Lord and Savior? Are any elements present that distract from the message? Make note of anything that distracts and plan to discuss it later with the team.

Now look at the room from the standpoint of singing in the congregation and listening to the Word of God preached. Sit silently. What do you hear? Do you hear noise, buzzing,

HVAC fan noise, echo, or reverb? Make notes on anything you observe. The space should be relatively quiet with no activity taking place in the room you are evaluating. What is the temperature of the space? Does the temperature change during the worship time? A change in temperature will affect the sound. Sound waves move faster through hot air than through cold air.[4]

Try talking aloud from your location. Better yet, if you are able, sing or have someone in your group sing. What do you hear? Is the room dead? Is there a lot of echo or noise? Does singing come naturally or do you strain? This is the starting point and will continue to be the point of reference for decisions about sound: how it is transmitted and how it is received by the listener.

You will remember from Chapter 3 on Authentic Worship that the entire congregation and the musicians and singers are performing before the Lord in worship. Each congregant (worshiper) must be able to hear more than the band. They must hear themselves sing as well as those around them.

Observe and Visualize Sound

I know the title doesn't make sense. How does one observe something that is invisible to the eye? How does one visualize a theme of nature that cannot be seen? If this seems too far off the grid, I encourage you to let me guide you through a process to facilitate a better understanding of the nature, function, and management of sound for worship. While some of the steps may seem juvenile, I believe if you perform the process outlined here, you will have a better understanding of how to build or modify a sound environment.

To start with, on a quiet day, when nothing is taking place in your sanctuary, stand in various places within the space (back, front, on stage, just forward of stage, and in the middle of the room). Clap your hands once. Listen. What do you hear? If there is no acoustical treatment, you will most likely hear echo (or reverb). It can be as pronounced as a "slap back" when the sound comes directly back at you after some amount of delay. The echo may come from one prominent location or maybe more than one.

Note the dominant echo and any subordinate echoes. Make a judgment about how long the echo lasts. If it is under one second, you are extremely fortunate. If it is longer than two seconds, acoustic adjustment is necessary. If the echo lasts exceptionally long, a great deal of work is needed, and the issues must be addressed prior to designing a sound system. This would be like the type of sound you hear in a cavernous space or mountain canyon. Again, note the observed time delay regarding the echo and the type of echo you heard in the various spots around the space.

Next, have someone stand in the front and speak. Can you hear them without amplification? What does it sound like? Walk around the room and sit in various locations and note how the sound may change. While this exercise may seem a bit much for a lay person, the experience you gain and the information you gather will help you understand and better communicate with the person performing the system design.

Even if the room sounds reasonably good, I strongly suggest you bring in a person who can evaluate the environment professionally using the proper equipment to make measurements. No room is perfect acoustically. All rooms have issues. If you can't afford one, as in our case, I will give you some basics that can be used to mitigate a few basic anomalies.

Fixer Upper

My church's worship room is a standard rectangle with parallel walls and a small amount of acoustic surface treatment. The building, like so many church buildings, was built over fifty years ago and modified along the way to update the look and feel. The basic framework is cinderblock walls, gyp-board covering, wall-to-wall carpeting, and a hard ceiling with fluorescent lights. The seating is removable, heavily padded chairs (which work well for the acoustics). The room is 50 feet long by 31 feet wide by 11 feet high and seats about 200 people. The stage area, extending off one end of the room, is roughly 18 feet by 18 feet. Last year, the bandleader and I decided to fix some of the troubling acoustics in the room. While I tried to hire a professional, I was not able to find one who would take on my project. I decided to apply what I knew about acoustics and fix the easiest problems.

For some time and prior to applying acoustical mitigations, the lead singer had complained that her voice was slapping back hard off the back wall and that she could not hear herself well on stage. The problems were greatest during rehearsal and less during worship time. When I stood in the middle of the room, I observed an obvious reverb and slap-back from the parallel walls. Also, in addition to the slap-back echo, a bass reverberation was in the room around 100 Hz. Both required mitigations. I have a fellow team member who is an AV professional like myself. We both have the requisite test gear to measure the room acoustics, which allowed us to document the acoustical issues.

The room acoustical treatments were simple. The local hardware store had a sale on Owens-Corning fiberglass two-by-four panels for about one-third the normal cost. We installed those on the back wall. The back wall slap-back nearly disappeared. Then we installed corner bass traps (designed to obsorb 80 to 120 Hz). Those bass traps have cleaned up some of the muddiness in the room. The drums now have a cleaner, more pronounced attack. More treatment is necessary, but this was a start.

Most church worship rooms have similar problems. While I do not suggest that the mitigations I used can be applied universally, these are examples of what can be accomplished without spending too much money. It is all too easy to get carried away, thinking that a totally dead space (e.g., absorption on all walls) is best. This would be a mistake. While valuable for a recording studio, a totally dead room sucks the life out of music in a live environment. Some reverb is necessary to provide some level of aural feedback for singers and a certain enhancement to the voices (aka singing in the shower).

Beware of Shiny Rocks[5] (Sound System Design)

If you have not already done so, this would be a good time to pull out your notes on worship and your goals for worship. The sound system must be a servant to all the requirements of worship and not drive those requirements.

There are a few, albeit idealized, sound system design goals. I list some of those here as reference as you work through the process. Keep in mind that any technical specification can be misleading if not published with all the data. The goal is not to purchase as big a system and as powerful (lots of watts of power) as you can afford. There are far more critical requirements than simply power.

Idealized Goals for Sound Design

An overarching goal for sound design is straightforward. A person's voice or an instrument should sound natural. That is to say, the tonal characteristics of the voice or instrument should sound the same if amplified or not. One of the processes I like to use to gauge whether I have achieved a natural sound or not is to mic a person and listen with the sound on and off. If the person sounds the same (tonally) with the sound on as they do with it off, then I have achieved the goal.

Idealized goals for sound design:

1. The same sound level (Sound Pressure Level – SPL) at every seat. You should pick the maximum or peak level SPL you will allow in the room. A typical maximum level for a small church would be under 100 dB SPL. Normal conversation occurs at around 75 to 80 dB SPL. More on this in the next chapter on the topic of loudness.

2. A "flat" frequency response at every seat. "Flat" in this case and in a typical room would be +/- 1.5 dB, 50 Hz to 20 KHz.[6] This may be tough to achieve but should be the goal.

3. Natural sound. An adage in the business is that the entire sound chain should be like a piece of wire—no distortion, coloration, or anomalies. A person's voice should sound just like their voice without amplification. An acoustical guitar should sound the same in the back of the room as it does when standing next to it.

4. Every component in the system is necessary to accomplish your worship goals. If components, processers, and extras are added, ask yourself, *Am I adding components and capabilities to help facilitate a better worship, or am I adding capability to satisfy industry hype or my own desires and ego?* Simpler is always better and easier to maintain as well.

5. The system must be simple enough to be operated by potential non-professionals without sacrificing quality.

At this point it would be good idea to bring in a professional sound designer. Your notes on the room environment (acoustics and tests) with your goals for the sound design and purpose are the materials you should have ready for the designer. Most commercial vendors will jump to talking about their product line (shiny rocks) and what they think you will need. It will take effort and patience to bring a vendor back to your set of requirements and your understanding of what is necessary for worship.

Chapter 9

Do You Need Assistance?

A friend of mine tells the story of getting a flat tire on highway 190 in the middle of Death Valley on a moonless night, years before the era of cell phones and OnStar. Though he is a well-organized person, he remembered struggling to find all the tools in the dark and then working to remove the flat and replace it in near pitch blackness. While he was in the middle of the changing the tire, an overwhelmingly bright light from high above enveloped him and the surrounding area. The light was so bright, he told me he first thought it was a sign. God had come to his rescue. Then, just as if heaven were speaking, he heard the authoritative words booming down to him, "Do you need assistance?"

Whether on a desert road in the middle of nowhere or in the sanctuary preparing for a worship service, it's okay to ask for and receive assistance. None of us are true experts. We learn constantly as we are being transformed by Christ and as we work our tradecraft. And if we were to admit it, while we savor being called "rock stars," we must admit that we stand on the shoulders of giants. Others have gone before to develop, perfect, and apply the physics, write the music, and develop the tech we enjoy applying today. And others will hopefully follow us—learning, applying, and worshiping.

When seeking a sound design professional, it starts with philosophy. Is the professional you want to hire familiar with the requirements of a worship service? Do they understand that the congregants must be able to hear themselves sing? Do they understand that the acoustical environment must be addressed first, and that work is followed by design, not the other way around? Do they peddle a certain brand, or are they brand agnostic? Can they pick the best product to meet your requirements and not draw you into upsell? Will they partner with you over time to develop a quality system—not just sales—with maintenance and upgrades? Do they genuinely care about your constraints and budget, and are they willing to work within those?

Who Can You Trust?

Several years ago, someone posted on Facebook a quote by Abraham Lincoln. He said, "Don't believe everything you read on the Internet just because there's a picture with a quote next to it." *Caveat Emptor* is Latin for "Let the buyer beware!" Beware of the shiny rocks! When researching sound, you will find a plethora of help and advice from every corner. Most of the information should be highly filtered and much can be ignored. Ask yourself a simple question. As you look for a professional and as you gather information, does the information apply to your church, your situation?[1] If not, ignore it. For instance, the sound design for a 1000 seat room does not apply to a 100- or 200-

seat room. The basic principles apply, the choice of equipment does not.

Vendor Relationship in a Hyper Sales-Driven World

Some of the best vendors I have ever worked with are those who when we first met, never discussed what they could sell me. They started a relationship by seeking to understand my work and the environment in which I work. Those vendors became long- term partners whom I depended upon for many, many years.

Characteristics of a trustworthy vendor[2]:

1. Will *listen* to you and honor the work you have done to understand and document the requirements for a sound system.[3]

2. Acknowledged and proven expertise in sound system design and communicates their understanding that the acoustic environment must be addressed before the system design.

3. Reputation/proven track record of working successfully with other churches your size. The company does not have to be Christian company. Simply look for the best you can afford. [Reference resources: SCN, Sound and Communications, etc.]

4. Holds to high standards of integrity and quality.

5. Is willing to partner with you over time and does not pursue in a "one-time" sale. Understands what that means. Many times, the budget will not allow for a

complete implementation of a design all at once. Seek a vendor who will help you with an implementation plan that can be achieved over a period and as budget allows.

6. Has a maintenance department that can service your equipment when needed with documented manufacturer relationships for best pricing and support after the sale.

7. Will work within your budget. Keep in mind, as a non-professional, you may greatly underestimate the costs associated with a sound system. When presented with the actual cost to achieve the requirements, you may suffer from sticker shock. Be willing to learn the actual costs associated with your requirements and be respectful of the vendor and their need to be in business.

A logical process follows establishing a relationship with a vendor. After you provide the requirements and talk those through, ask the vendor to provide you with a rough design and a Rough Order of Magnitude (ROM) cost for the project. A ROM should be turned around quickly and provides a budgetary number that is usually +/- 20% of the final quote. By not doing a complete design up front, both you and the vendor can gauge whether both of you are on the same page. This is where, if needed, negotiation and compromise may take place.

If the ROM meets requirements and is within boundaries, you can move into the formal design process. If not, choices will have to be made regarding scope, complexity, and selection of equipment. Take your time in the step. If compromises must take place to conform to budget, make sure you are compromising in areas that will not severely affect the listener/congregant (positive and negatively affecting compromises).

Once a system and budget are determined, the next phase will be for formal design and scope of work. Ask the vendor to supply a list of deliverables and the expected performance level from the sound system. Always keep in mind, you are not assembling a bunch of high-tech equipment for simply the enjoyment of such. You are designing a system to be used for corporate worship by the body of Christ.

Once you agree with the vendor on a timeline for the purchase, installation, testing, and tuning of the system, the project can start. If you are the one responsible for the project, I encourage you, as much as you are able and within your power to do so, be involved in each step of the project. Try to understand what the vendor is doing and why. In this manner, you should have no surprises when the system is complete. All issues should be vetted during the project instead of waiting to the end when traditionally there is a huge "punch list" of things to fix.

One caution about the final stages of test and "ringing out" the system. It's best not to rush this part of the project. The temptation is to start using the system before it is completely tested and adjusted. Resist the temptation. I know of many clients who have expressed dissatisfaction with an installation because they used the system early, found problems with equipment not working right, and pre-judged the entire project based on a bad experience that did not represent the real experience.

Can You Hear Me? First Test

When the sound system is complete, it is a good idea to perform some simple tests. These tests will help you understand the quality and the limitations of your new sound system. Start by standing on the stage next to the musical instruments. Listen to each one individually. Note the sound, the timbre, the nuance. The natural sound that you hear from the instrument is the sound that you want to amplify. Chris Mitchell who serves as FOH engineer for the popular rock band, Umphrey's McGee, says that his goal is to build a very natural sound from each of the instruments through the sound system, rather than using extensive EQ to modify the sound.

When talking about the drums in particular, he says that this is "how I think about my drum mix now: it should be just like standing in front of the kit, at whatever volume I desire."[4] Whether you have a musician or tech who understands the process of equalization applied to each instrument to enhance the instruments sound, the starting point is simply, what does the voice or instrument sound like unamplified, naturally?

Base the evaluation of the sound system upon the natural versus amplified sound of speech, singing, instruments, etc. I encourage you to minimize the use of equalization. Work with the vendor and sound professional to make the changes necessary to bring a natural sound to the room.

Questions: Are you and your team prepared to spend the time and the effort necessary to guarantee that the sound system addresses the biblical requirements for worship

Chapter 10

It's "Not" Rocket Science

(Managing the Front of House)

"Mixing sound in the live realm is not rocket science. In fact, it's probably closer to voodoo" (Dave Rat, FOH engineer, Rat Sound).

"It's way easier to please 10,000 people than five musicians" (Sean Sturge, monitor engineer).

Prepare to Be Prepared

Front of House mix for worship is not the same as mixing a concert, though in some churches it's hard to tell the difference. In the worship service, the FOH serves one purpose and one purpose only—the worship of God. Everything else is subservient to the main purpose. The worship service is not a place for any upfront sound or magic. It is simple, straightforward, Christ-honoring sound. This is the place to learn the discipline of not being swept away by the latest plug-in, the latest style or nuance. This is where the music is played, presented, and mixed in a manner that allow others to follow and to sing!

The process starts with proper planning and preparation. Being prepared means that the music is rehearsed with the FOH for that week. Rehearsals with the entire team means that there is less stress on Sundays. It means that the entire team (e.g., music leader, musicians, singers, tech crew, and pastors) all know the music, timing, and sequence of events for the worship service. The process, though, is more than the mechanics.

We found a significant change in our worship services when the bandleader started having devotions before Wednesday night rehearsal, with prayer that night and before the services. All the band members pray for the services every service. And changes have happened. People started singing louder and louder. Now the congregation is singing so well I hear it in the back of the room at the booth. Sometimes the singing is so good, the congregation overwhelms the band. It is pure delight when that happens.

***Mixology*[1]**

The goal of a good mix for worship is simple: all instruments and vocals blend in a manner that the congregation can sing with. There is no other purpose. If the congregation cannot sing, worship is inhibited. If the band dominates, the worship may shift to the created thing.

There are times in the life of a team (musicians and techs) when the music elevates off the page. During these moments, the sound of each instrument and vocal is fully articulated, nuanced, and a delight to listen and sing with. In smaller church venues, those moments may be rare. While we may think that those unique moments are the goal of our work, they are not. The goal is to achieve a sound that can be fully entered into. It must promote worship!

Mixology is the process of bringing all the essential elements of the mix together to build a FOH mix for worship. Mixology includes selecting proper microphones and interfaces for the vocals and instruments being used. It includes building a monitor mix that supports the band's requirements and then building a house mix that works for the venue. Included is attention to the detail of sound levels, musical mixing, and a continued attention to all that is taking place during the worship service.

Many good references can be found both online and in book form that cover the topic of mixology very well. The discussion here is not exhaustive but merely suggestive of the key areas for thought and attention. While mixology is an especially important part of the work of a FOH, I am only covering it from the standpoint of a non-professional in a small venue.

The work of building a mix takes time and energy from all who participate. The learning process never stops. If you stop learning, it is an indication that it is time to step aside and let others serve in your place.

Start at the beginning (always).

When building a mix for the first time or when changes have been made in the band, it is best to start with all equalization and effects turned off. I have a personal preference to keep the mix for worship simple. Listen to the gain structure of each instrument, adjusting first the input levels of each vocal and instrument routed through the console. When the input is set without clipping, adjust the board level to match expectation on the sound required. Then build the mix. The trend (a welcomed trend from this author) is to keep equalization (EQ) and special effects to an absolute minimum. In doing so, the most natural sound of each voice and instrument will be presented.[2]

Early in my audio career, while attending a well-known sound design seminar, I sat next to the FOH for a famous singer/group at the time. I had the opportunity to ask anything I wanted about how to mix for a top ten, high-profile performer. The key takeaway from the conversations was (among many other things), if it doesn't happen on stage for the performer, the performance doesn't happen. This is purely a worldly perspective on music performance, but it points to a key principle in FOH mixing—the monitor mix is the start and end for the musician.

Before setting the FOH mic for a worship service, start with the stage monitor mix. The monitor mix will have a direct impact on the FOH mix. If the monitor mix is too loud, that volume in most venues will drive the house volume. Sometimes the monitor mix can get so loud (based on requests from musicians to raise the monitor mix level) it can overwhelm the FOH mix. I often demonstrate the problem by turning off the house mix and asking the bandleader to listen. If the monitor mix fills the room, the monitor mix is too loud.

I also like to do something I see few FOH doing. I stand on stage with the vocalists and musicians and listen to the monitor mix from their perspective.[3] Then I can better understand their needs and how their requests work into not only the monitor mix, but the house mix as well. Digital mixing consoles have a cool feature that allows any mix to be managed on a pad or a smartphone. Using a pad for the monitor mix keeps the FOH from running back and forth to the console.

I encourage musicians to exercise patience during the monitor and house mix setup process. Allow the FOH time to listen and make the needed adjustments, especially in the smaller venues where there may be only one person working sound. Sometimes it's easy to start playing and ask, "Am I *on* out there?" For FOH it is vital that you patiently work through the process of setting levels. It's not easy to wait when you are ready to play or sing. But if you follow this systematically, you will achieve the kind of results you desire.

Since most of the music we sing in church today is based on the rock-n-roll band with drums, bass guitar, acoustic and electric guitars, piano and/or synth, and vocals, the proper place to start to achieve a good balance, both on stage and in the house, is with the drums. The drum volume sets the volume for all other instruments, and it is important that the drummer understand this basic principle. The drummer should be able to play based on this principle.

Layer the Sound

We manage the drums uncaged with only a minimum boost from microphones (kick and cymbals). When uncaged, the punch, the dynamics, and the nuance are relevant and present—unlike the rather wimpy sound of an electronic drum set. Caging acoustic drums is roughly akin to caging a wild beast. You will not know the depth of the sound unless the drums are uncaged but tamed. The beast when tamed and nuanced provides a richly layered sound that stands in stark contrast to an isolated and purely amplified sound.

Uncaging the drums requires a drummer who is not only able but also willing to tame the beast. While the taming process is taught in professional classes and conservatories (I am admonished by my professionally trained musician friends on this point), self-taught drummers typically are unaware of the requirements of taming. Our bandleader and drummer, has worked the taming process his entire career from heavy-metal band to church band. He taught me the process of restraint and blend with the drums, rather than allowing the drums to dominate all other instruments. He plays as though his elbows are glued to his waist. The result is nothing less than wonderful.

The mix starts with the drums. The bass is layered to compliment the drummer and not overwhelmed with an overdriven bass line. Once those two levels are set for the stage monitor mix and the house, move then to the acoustic then electric guitar. Add the piano or synth (and other instruments) to build the base line for the vocalists. Once the instruments are in balance, add the vocals to the mix.

When developing the overall mix for worship, I operate under the philosophy that the lead vocalist is the most important sound for the congregation to hear. The congregation follows the lead vocalist for pitch, timing, and words. The mix therefore is *not* the same as it would be for a concert or a recording. In fact, I have been criticized for not bringing the vocals into a referenced recorded album mix. I resist the tendency. When an album is mixed in such a manner, the words of the song cannot be easily determined. This should not be the case since it causes a struggle in congregational worship.

While I will describe more about sound levels in a forthcoming section, most of the music used in worship services today sounds poor, and in fact, wimpy unless played at a certain level. A meticulously designed sound system will support good, strong levels without being so loud as to cause an offense. I encourage the reader to develop strong, solid mixes that present the intended sound properly mixed and at a proper level.

Consistent Mixology

Early in my career as FOH, I was frustrated when the Sunday morning mix did not match the rehearsal mix. Rehearsals provide valuable time for both the musicians to work through the music and for the FOH to build the sound for the upcoming service. In our situation we have two rehearsals—Wednesday night and Sunday before the first worship service. These are complete rehearsals with every song being practiced in its entirety. Most of the time the rehearsal mix and service mix are not the same. It is most likely a false impression that they should be. The dynamics of the room change from rehearsal to service, and band members rarely play the same in worship as in rehearsal.

It is important to be aware of changes and be prepared to make the necessary adjustments for both the monitor and house mix. I believe it is wrong thinking to "set it and forget it." Mixology demands attention to detail. Mixology is dynamic, not static, mixing. I want to be careful here to make sure that dynamic mixing is understood. Dynamic mixing is working the console so that the house mix is balanced and appropriate for the music played. It is not about the FOH interpreting the music to build dynamics in the mix. This would involve giving more or less prominence to a particular instrument in an effort to build fullness when that prominence is not intended in the music or by the music leader.

Mute!

The mute button is your friend. At the same time, most pastors distrust the mute. Or more to the point, distrust the FOH running the mute. For the mute button to be your friend, to be useful, you must earn the pastor's (and musician's) trust and respect. And not miss a beat. Every new pastor I work with wants to control the power button on their wireless microphone. When I tell them, "I want the wireless transmitter on at all times," they look at me in disbelief and usually say emphatically, "No!" Truth be told, pastors are not thinking about turning their microphones on and off when they step up to preach. They are thinking, and rightly so, about the sermon. It is our job to make sure they can be heard.

Riding the mute button for the pastor and for the music team takes a lot of attention. The outcome, though, is cleaner and much more professional. I have trained our team to ride the microphone mute during communion, which is not easily accomplished. We need to hear everything the pastor is saying about the elements, but we should not hear him chewing or swallowing.

One of the greatest fears a pastor has is that the microphone will be on when he goes to the bathroom. This is a genuine concern. That is why is it vital that getting into a rhythm of muting and unmuting is important.

Most consoles allow the grouping of mutes so that the pastors, vocalists, and musicians can all be muted with one button or a selection of a few, rather than trying to hit many at one time. When used correctly, the sound is seamless. When not used or not paid attention to, the sound can be a disaster.

Attention Paid Is Attention Earned

One Sunday morning, I was waiting for the pastor to start the service. Rather than visiting with friends, I keep my attention on what is going with the musicians and the team while watching for the pastor to walk to the front and welcome the congregation. On this morning, I was watching the pastor, but just as he walked forward, a friend came to the front of the console to say hi and blocked my view. I apologized and told him I had to see/watch the pastor. My friend immediately stepped aside and said, "Oh, that's right. You have a system." His comment made me smile. He understood that I was disciplined in my service and distractions interrupted the flow of the service. Thank you.

For me, one of the worst things that can happen in a service is for the pastor to ask the audience, "Is my mike on? Can you hear me?" Or for a musician to tap, tap, tap, and blow into the microphone (please don't do this—it will ruin the mic) because they are not confident the mic is on. That should never be the case. The microphones should be on when needed and muted when not.

Listen. Again, I Say Listen.

The bulk of the sound comes from the ability to simply put together a good mix. "A tech with a lot of skill and mediocre equipment will always sound better than one with low skill and the best gear."[4]

LBWA

The only way that you will fully understand the FOH mix is by what I call LBWA – Listening by Walking Around.[5] One of the very first exercises for a potential FHO is to sit in various locations in the auditorium and listen both in the rehearsal and service. Again, as always, listening and increasing listening skills is vital to performing a credible FOH. Many times, I get puzzled looks. The response is, "Why don't you just show me how to push the buttons and move those things that move up and down."

I insist the candidate listen to the service first—not casually but actively. After each time (more than once), I ask the question, "Tell me what you heard." If the response is, "I don't know what you are talking about," then I explain. "What instruments did you hear? How were they mixed? Did any of the sound seem unbalanced? Was it natural?"

If the response at this point is, "I still don't know what you are talking about," then I tell them they are not ready for FOH. I can train for listening better, but if at the beginning there is no insight into sound and how sounds should sound and mix, then the amount of work is sometimes too great.

Even after being trained on FOH for some time, I still insist that our FOH get out of the booth and walk around. I do so during rehearsal and during the service. Keep in mind, few mixing locations are ideal. Having a mixing console that sits in the same acoustical location (profile) as those in the audience is unusual, so it is vital to occasionally listen to what the audience hears. Many improvements to the overall mix have been achieved by this simple activity.

Hurting Ears

There are absolute limits that should be observed regarding the sound level in the room. OSHA guidelines say that at 120 dB[6] SPL[7] (Sound Pressure Level), the threshold of pain has been reached. This means damage to the listeners' ears is taking place at 120 dB and above. While much of the music that is played today requires high levels, for most venues, I suggest between 85 and 95 dB maximum, mid-house. Normal conversation takes place at around 80 dB. If you are in a room that seats around 200 to 400 people, 90 dB is very loud. The best policy for the small venue is to limit the level presented in the room.

Damaging Sound

Collateral damage is not unique to the military. It happens on many Sunday mornings when a FOH is sleeping or on the phone. It happens with a musician who has not practiced the music and is gleefully playing off-key. An off-key vocalist is even more disturbing. In my history of FOH, I have experienced the damage and have been a party to adding to such. A normal response is to fix the problem. Get rid of it. Move on. Off- key guitar playing (oops—capo was not set) or an FOH asleep at the wheel is disruptive and annoying. For the most part, I have trained our FOH to turn down or turn off any instrument that is not on key. While it may anger the musician, the off-putting sound may significantly disrupt congregational singing.

Mic-ology

Recently a guest speaker came to our church to speak on a special program that takes place at our church facility. He came at the very last minute, immediately before the beginning of the service, with a computer to plug into our projector. I dealt with the computer issue. We scrambled to get his presentation into a form that could be presented, and after we did so, with little time to spare, I instructed him on which microphone to use. I told him to hold the mic close to his mouth and speak in a normal tone. He said he understood perfectly.

Just before he was asked to speak, I again reminded him of the microphone etiquette "to be heard clearly!" As he walked on stage, he completely ignored the microphone. At that point, the pastor asked him to pick up the wireless mic, which he did. As he stood at the podium, he said, while holding the microphone at his waist, "You all can hear, right?" Someone said yes, and those in the back of the sanctuary mumbled no. I signaled to him a gestured to use the mic and hold it close to his mouth. He lifted the mic to his waist and started talking. I raised the mic level to hear him, and then he thrust the mic to his mouth, causing feedback, which began the cycle of too loud, too soft, too loud. Finally, it settled, but the speaker struggled to hold the microphone in any one place.

This story may sound overly critical. That is not my intent. Most people are not professional speakers. We ask people to speak who have had no formal training and are nervous to begin with. I understand that. My point, though, is that even professional speakers have done the same routine. Pastors routinely say, "I don't need a microphone, my voice is strong." The voice may be strong enough when they think about it, but invariably, if a speaker drops their voice for emphasis, the congregation will miss the words and miss the message.

One of my greatest challenges and frustrations is the misuse and abuse of microphones. First and foremost, I have a philosophy about being heard clearly and precisely in worship. If you are speaking in a worship service, then you must have something to say that contributes to the worship service. If you cannot be heard, then the contribution is all for nothing. It is a waste of time! I work hard to train anyone and everyone who is going to speak at our worship service. I am successful only about fifty percent of the time. I am persistent.

Tap! Tap! Tap!

Please don't. Tapping can damage the microphone. Do not blow into a microphone to test whether it is on or not. Simply speak into the microphone at a normal speaking level.

Trust the FOH to adjust the volume. If the FOH is doing their job, there is no need for tapping or saying, "Can you all hear me?"

I Am Last

The older I get, the more I am aware that most of what I have learned and am able to do, I have learned from others. I stand on the shoulders of others who have either taken the time and showed me how or have allowed me to observe them. As we labor in the church, we are challenged with our own lack of confidence, overly developed confidence, or outright ego.

We tend to protect our area of ministry and what we know for one of two reasons: we don't want others to know how little we really do know, or we want to protect our skill so our influence and contribution is not taken away by someone else. Both attitudes have no place in the body of Christ. As explored in the chapter on gifts, we have been given gifts and talents and skills to serve the body, and not for our own self-aggrandizement, our selfish purpose. John the Baptist said, "I must decrease, and He must increase" (John 3:30). It's a good reminder to consistently and constantly diminish our view of ourselves, bringing all things under the authority and into the service of Christ.

Therefore, all involved in worship must be open and willing to mentor and teach others in the process. I encourage the reader to use every opportunity as it arises as a teaching moment both for the gospel and for the skills.

Questions: As a member of the band or sound team, do you find yourself pulling out your phone as soon as there is opportunity? Would you rather check email and chats than listen to the sermon? What practical steps can you take to reduce the influence of your phone, especially during the worship service? Is technology driving your decisions, or are you the master of the tech you use? How would the decisions regarding technology and the use of it in worship be different if you were the master?

PART IV

Seduction

(Bringing technology in submission to the gospel of Jesus Christ)

"It has become appallingly obvious that our technology has exceeded our humanity" (Albert Einstein).

Introduction to Part IV

While preparing the manuscript for this book, I was asked why I included a section on the future of technology in a book on the sounds of worship. The view is that the future of technology and especially Artificial Intelligence (AI) should be discussed elsewhere. It is important for the reader to understand the pervasive and at times insidious nature of technology and its impact on our daily lives and as related to the topic in the book – worship. The simple addition of a sound reinforcement system (technology) to the worship service was originally well intended. But the decision followed the conventional wisdom of the Law of Unintended Consequences. Many now believe a worship service cannot take place without sound reinforcement and video projection. We struggle with the false impression that if the sound system or media system fails, we will not have a proper worship service. It is therefore incumbent on all involved to understand the nature of the very thing we believe we are dependent upon.

In this section, I draw attention to the pervasive infusion of technology into our lives and the warning signs that point to a trend in which the technology is ruling over us, rather than the other way around. My intent is not to frighten the reader, even though some of the greatest minds (such as Stephen Hawking) were deeply disturbed over the implications that are summarized here. This is no small matter or one that has little implication for the church. The power behind and in technology can overwhelm us if we do not prayerfully and carefully consider our application of technological solutions. It is vital we understand both the good and the bad that flows from of its use.

Chapter 11

Who Will Stop the Train?

"Technology is anything that wasn't around when you were born" (Alan Kay, Computer Scientist).

"Any sufficiently advanced technology is equivalent to magic" (Arthur C. Clarke).

"The real danger is not that computers will begin to think like men, but that men will begin to think like computers" (Sydney Harris, Journalist).

When Computers Best Humans

Several years ago, Ken Jennings made a career of being a know-it-all with a record-breaking winning streak on the television trivia game show *Jeopardy!*. Jennings was famous and almost impossible to beat. Though he did eventually lose on *Jeopardy!*, he made an astounding seventy-five appearance/wins amassing a total of $3,522,700 in cash.[1]

As *Jeopardy!* viewership skyrocketed, Jennings came to the attention of the Artificial Intelligence (AI) scientists at IBM. They saw a live target that would provide a way to demonstrate AI's capabilities and yes, superiority. IBM believed they could beat Jennings at his own game.

Jennings in contrast was convinced no machine could best him. No machine could fully understand the nuance, double meanings, and oblique references of the English language. Send in Watson.

IBM built Watson for the exact purpose of proving Jennings wrong. "Watson is a question-answering computer system capable of answering questions posed in natural language, developed in IBM's DeepQA project . . . Watson was named after IBM's founder and first CEO, industrialist Thomas J. Watson."[2] In 2011, Watson paired off with *Jeopardy!* icons Ken Jennings and Brad Rutter. Watson easily bested both Jennings and Rutter, winning the one million-dollar prize. The machine dominated the game and dominated Jennings thoughts about it in the years to follow.

In 2013, Jennings was featured in a TED[3] talk. In his talk, he explains how he grew up enjoying knowing information that others did not know. He came to an intoxicating conclusion early in life that knowledge is power. Given his mindset for trivia, Jennings was a natural for the *Jeopardy!* show, and he enjoyed every minute of the game. In fact, he says he would have played for free—it was that fun. When Watson defeated him soundly, however, the tables turned, and Jennings was not the least bit happy about his loss. He now promotes himself as the "Obsolete Know-It-All" with a cautious view of AI.

Watson is not the only AI machine to best humans in a game. AlphaGo, an AI program designed by a UK startup and now owned by Google, designed a computer program to play the board game GO. GO is a 2,500-year-old game of strategy that uses a nineteen square by nineteen square board with black and white "stones."

The goal is for one player to surround the other's territory and thus win the game. While not well known in the US, GO[4] is the oldest board game still being played today. In October 2015, in a highly promoted and publicized tournament, AlphGO won four out of five rounds while playing international champion Lee Sodel. The loss shook Sodel to the core. He had never lost a game. This loss was significantly more painful than if Sodel had lost to a human. The loss was to a machine.

Technology has permeated every aspect of our lives. The beast has been loosed, not easily tamed, and certainly not squeezed back in the bottle. The hybrid vehicle that I just purchased is touted as having over 50 computers, 100 million lines of code[5], and over a dozen network protocols used to manage the car and the smarts to make driving decisions before I ever realize they need to be made. The stuff of science fiction is here.

It's no longer a dream to talk to your computer—even if we don't call it a computer anymore. Siri, Alexa, etc., are at my beck and call. In fact, as recently reported by Apple computer, Siri is listening even when we think "she"[6] is not listening. She hears many of the words we thought were private. She records those words. She analyzes those words. Ostensibly Siri is listening to provide better service and to gain a better understanding of us—our preferences and desires—or so the designers say. As you may already know, the "throw away" words we speak are recorded and documented. This overarching invasion into our private world is unprecedented, yet we generally accept the tools and devices as convenient or even necessary for life.

In a TED talk, Jennings says this as trend that must be reversed. Not that we can stop all AI work, but that we humans must strive to keep learning and stretching our brain. In Jennings's talk, he mentioned that the part of the brain that works spatial relationships, the posterior parietal cortex (PPC), is shrinking dramatically in those who depend on GPS for navigation. Brain shrinkage is a serious issue. If we understood the devastating effect technology has on our brain and well-being, we might be more cautious in how we use and depend upon it. Jennings also makes the point that just because you can look something up through Google (or ask Siri), it does not mean that you know something.

The sum of the world's information is doubling every eighteen months. That means that in the last year and a half, the total information on any topic is more than any time in human history. We are buried in information. That fact raises an important question I ask often: Whom do you trust for accurate information, and where do you find it? The answer to that question is elusive. Technology, for the good or for the bad it brings, is making the quest for truth quite difficult.

Technology on the Rise

I will never forget that day in the early 1982 when I purchased my first computer. While I wanted a personal computer for many reasons, the main reason was for word processing. For most of my life I hated my handwriting, which is not pretty. It is irregular and difficult to decipher at times, even for me. So, when word processing boldly entered the stage, I embraced it—spell check and all. I started with an Osborne[7] transportable. The computer was an early "portable" computer but much too bulky to lug around. It sported a tiny five-inch black and white screen, hardly a comfortable size for efficient word processing. It wasn't cheap ($2,500 in 1982 dollars and over $6K in today's dollars), but it worked. It wasn't long before a twelve-inch screen was attached, and composition was easier.

Finally I could write without huge black sections of marked-up pages of typewriter text, and without the pain of mis-typing and whiting out letters, only to see that the page became misaligned in the process of correction and now nothing was aligned. Time to start over. Gone were the days of completing an entire manuscript to realize that one word (used throughout) was savagely misspelled. The entire labor of producing a manuscript was lost. With word processing, I have no more embarrassment from others struggling to read my writing or suggesting I take a typing class.

My desire, or even rush, to adopt tech has been a fire

burning since childhood. My father had encouraged me to enter the field of electronics and did everything he could to advance my knowledge and experience with tubes, resistors, capacitors, transformers, and the new transistors. He was the head of the science department for the elementary school district in which we lived. Dad passionately believed that a career in electronics would pay far more than a career in teaching, and especially more than any call to ministry.[8] Even though my father was a highly successful science teacher, whom many still remember and talk of fondly, he was never completely happy with his lot in life.

With Dad's coaching and prodding, electronics became the center of all my endeavors. It still is. I have come to realize the burn for ever-increasing tech ability and capability has not always served me well. In fact, it has brought me to a state where I now question the very projects and technological developments that I have sought in life. The seduction of tech is powerful. There is a rush, a certain high associated with researching and purchasing and installing the latest gear, or any gear for that matter. Or in solving a complex technical problem.

These days, it is not only the techno-nerds[9] like me who hear and follow the technological siren's seductive call. It seems the whole of the world is enslaved. The enslavement has made Apple the most valuable company on earth—more valuable than any medical, food service, or humanitarian organization in the world. Can I live without my iPhone? Can I function in a meaningful way every day without it? My phone is with me everywhere I go, and it doesn't just tag along.

The smartphone is drastically better than the obsolete typewriter and the ancient fountain pen or the clunky dial-up phone. The new phone is a powerful computer that can perform complex tasks that just a few years ago took many devices to achieve. The phone is my personal always-on connection to the rest of the world.

Generally, we have assumed that the digital world is a God-given act of grace to allow us better lives. Life in the twenty-first century is indeed an easier life, with all the conveniences, than I had when growing up. The transformation of the last fifty years is nothing short of astonishing, and to be honest, overwhelming. The fact that we have technology in abundance, though, does not necessarily mean it is God-given or God- intended. The tsunami of high-tech gadgets and options that pour over us daily can and does make us numb to the realities of living.

Though my iPhone is my companion, I find myself nostalgic for my typewriter (thrown away years ago) and my fountain pen (dried up, forgotten, and resting in a heap of other pens). I am not a Luddite (English workers in the 19th century who destroyed machinery because it threatened their jobs)! Technology is extremely useful. You can confirm this with my wife—I consume a great deal of it.

The typewriter, however, did not enslave by demanding I attend to it every few minutes. The typewriter did not ring (or ding) to announce itself (except on carriage returns) and tell me that it had something crucial for me to look at. It sat quietly, unassuming, not attracting attention to itself. I did not drag it everywhere I went (an odd image).[10] Neither did the fountain pen call attention to itself. It never shouted at me. Those objects, in proper relationship to man, waited subdued on the sidelines to be used when needed. Conversely, the iPhone suffers from a profound case of attention deficit disorder.

Digital, Digital Everywhere

We are now a fully digitized culture. Changed. Transformed from a society of touch, feel, and substance, to a culture of the virtual. The untouchable. The not real. We are hyperbolically connected and yet strangely disconnected from each other and from the realities of life. Paper money is no longer preferred. A face-to-face interpersonal relationship is too complicated. It's messy. It's far easier to post a feel-good one-liner online than to wade through messy and complicated in-person relationships. One's value is ranked by the number of their followers on Twitter, or the number of likes to a post on Facebook, or so many stars on Yelp. Character and integrity matter little.

The shift from analog to digital occurred many years ago. In 1991, Western Society moved from the Industrial Revolution to the Information Revolution. In that year, the number of information or knowledge workers were more than traditional factory workers. The scale had tipped.[11]

The rush of tech and the overflow of new and improved gadgets can numb us to the reality of technology's profound effect on the way we function in life. Marshall McLuhan proposed in *The Medium Is the Message* that "A medium itself, not the content it carries, . . . affects the society in which it plays a role not only by the content delivered over the medium, but also by the characteristics of the medium itself."[12] The medium (e.g., the smartphone) changes, modifies, alters the user in a manner that is not expected or necessarily predictable. Those alterations deeply affect the way the individual lives and how the individual perceives life.

In other words, as soon as we employ technology, our perception of reality is altered. We don't realize it, and maybe we don't care. While we may believe that technology is a good thing, the downside of the use of computers and smartphones are manifold. Psychologists have noted a critical impact on our lives in the forms of wasted time, loss of concentration, a threat to human health, personal isolation, lack of privacy, stress, poor sleep habits, and addiction.[13]

I recall standing directly next to IBM's new quantum computer and marveling at its beauty. It was outside its super-cold environment (-270 degrees Celsius /.015 Kelvin) that the computer requires in order to function. Outside its cocoon, all the beautiful and intricate detail could easily be observed and admired. The computer looked more like an elegant gold chandelier than a device that could solve complex equations. I was told by the expert standing in front of me that the IBM quantum computer could solve in a few minutes what would take today's super computers hundreds of years to solve.[14]

The quantum computer functions in ways that boggle the mind. A qubit (quantum bit) can be either a one or zero at the same time. How is that possible? The IBM on display was rated at 50 qubits. Experts say that at 100 qubits, a quantum computer would be more powerful than all the supercomputers on the earth combined.[15] The input/output (I/O) is handled via microwave wave guides that do not touch the substrate. The plethora of waveguides attached to the quantum device are what give the computer the look of a chandelier. I recall being rather excited when the IBM representative invited me to New Jersey to join a team learning how to program the new beast.

Quantum computers present huge challenges for society. These will rapidly become the new mainframes of the computational world. Quantum computers will be able to handle the most complex calculations known to man, including simulations of the brain and of life. Resequencing human DNA will be child's play.

AI Ubiquity

We are at the same time challenged by automation and AI. AI as a program differs fundamentally from most computer programs. Prior to AI, computers were programmed to perform certain tasks in a certain manner, in a sequence of exact line by line commands over and over, without changes and hopefully with no errors. A change in the requirement of the program meant that the program itself had to be modified or rewritten.

With AI, the program is designed to learn in a manner like the way humans learn (though currently at a very crude level compared to humans). If a change in the operation of an AI computer is needed, it can make the changes by reprogramming itself and adapting to the new environment. AI is at the heart of self-driving cars and IBM's Watson, the computer that beat Ken Jennings, and the core of AlphaGO, the machine that beat the world champion in the game GO.

As I write this manuscript, I am very aware of the AI behind the word processing program. The program alerts me to misspelled words, grammatical errors, and punctuation problems. It's handy. It makes editing a little better, but it doesn't catch everything. Sometimes the grammar checker simply does not understand the message I am conveying, yet it is there. Ever present. Monitoring my every keystroke. On a grander scale, "there is now hope that [AI] will be able to diagnose deadly diseases, make million-dollar trading decisions, and do countless other things to transform whole industries. But this won't happen—or shouldn't happen—unless we find ways of making techniques like deep learning more understandable to their creators and accountable to their users.[16] Otherwise, it will be hard to predict when failures might occur—and it's inevitable they will."[17]

The transformation of tech is now so rapid, we will face the challenge of smartphones rapidly being considered obsolete.[18] Within a few years, a far greater personal computing power will be available in the form of eyeglasses that can project the computer images directly on the retina of the eye of a person wearing those glasses. With direct connection to the internet (via the new 5G networks or metro Wi-Fi), an infinite amount of data will be available to be streamed to the eye/brain while overlaying that data on the world around us. The glasses will use ubiquitous AI to know and understand our behaviors and modify how they operate based on our personal preferences. Imagine the worship service where parishioners are asked to remove their glasses rather than "silencing their phone." In worship, it would be nearly impossible to tell if a member of the congregation was Tweeting or reading Facebook posts or fully worshiping.

From retina projection to direct brain interface is perhaps a shorter leap. Sensor caps are already available that provide input and output directly from the brain. No need for buttons or screens or glasses. Information can flow freely from brain to internet and back again or to other people. If someone wants to know your thoughts, you just think it. No barriers. No firewall. Watson?[19] Our attraction to high-tech is tempered by our frustration. Often I feel as if I should and can master it. Control it. Make it work for me. But it has a mind of its own. At times, the phrase "mind of its own" is not euphemistic.

A further implication for the church is one we are not taking seriously. With a greater computational power available, there is a tendency to depend on the technology to do the work that we should be doing. Computer programs can model an acoustic environment and provide solutions. The old Dolby Labs studio on Pateros in San Francisco developed the capability to adjust the studio acoustic characteristics depending on use (e.g., movie, speaker/lecture, concert). The environment was manually selected. Meyers Sound Lab Galileo does this automatically. With quantum computing, programs could simulate environments in real-time and dynamically and accurately adjust the real environment making for a perfect sound at every seat in the house during music and during preaching.

The challenge becomes not so much the fact that we can achieve a better environment for the listener, but rather that we would depend upon the technology to the point of removing the human factors from the process. Fewer and fewer people today understand the basics of sound, the physics. The reliance on technology to a greater degree removes the need to know and understand how sound works—indeed how everything works or should work. If we depend solely on technology, we give up the ability to make the decisions we should be making as stewards of worship in bringing all things under our control.

There exists the possibility of using AI within a worship service to maximize the intended response to the music or the message. AI could be used to fine tune a mix, adjust the lights, temperature, and introduce aromas that would trigger a favorable response – whatever the predetermined response may be.

Technology in Submission

"If we continue to develop our technology without wisdom or prudence, our servant may prove to be our executioner" (Omar Bradley, General, US Army).

"The Sabbath was made for man, not man for the Sabbath" (Mark 2:27).

It was Saturday, Sabbath. Jesus and the disciples were hungry. They needed food, so they gleaned what they could from harvested fields. Immediately Jesus came under the watchful eyes and insidious criticism of the Pharisees (the Jewish religious leaders). Jewish law stated that no work could be performed on Saturday. The Sabbath was holy unto the Lord.[20] Jesus responded to the Pharisees with clarity. The Sabbath was for man, not the other way around. When Jesus declared the relationship of the sacred Sabbath and man, He was making clear that all things (other than human) were to serve man—not the other way around.

The Jewish leaders practiced and preached the opposite and had established a pattern of life that was nearly impossible for ordinary people to live by. The leaders had written law that added to the law of God and stated that keeping the Sabbath holy (e.g., set apart) meant that no physical work whatsoever could take place. The law was arbitrary and unnecessarily burdensome for the poor who had to work daily just to meet the necessities of life. In this manner, the Jewish authorities declared themselves more righteous than others simply because they religiously followed the rules of the law. Jesus easily dismissed the leaders' laws by declaring God's relationship of man and the Sabbath.

More importantly, immediately following the creation of man and woman, God commanded man to have dominion over all the earth. God blessed them and said to them, "Be fruitful and increase in number; fill the earth and *subdue it, and rule over* the fish in the sea and the birds in the sky and over every living creature that moves on the ground" (Genesis 1:28, emphasis added).

In the domain of earth, God has given mankind the responsibility to be stewards of creation and subdue every living creature and all things physical. In other words, do not let the earth or the creatures of earth or anything of the earth have dominion over you. Be a slave[21] to no creature or thing on earth. Our responsibility is to bring all things under the authority of Christ. This is our challenge as it relates to the sounds of worship.

Practical Submission

The very ones who market their high-tech gadgets to us understand to some degree the correct relationship between tech and their households and their children. When Steve Jobs was asked how his kids liked having iPhones and iPads, he replied that he would not let them have either. Jobs, like several Silicon Valley executives, subscribed to a form of education that does not depend on electronics and computers.

"Research has found that an eighth-grader's risk for depression jumps 27% when he or she frequently uses social media. Kids who use their phones for at least three hours a day are much more likely to be suicidal. And recent research has found the teen suicide rate in the US now eclipses the homicide rate, with smartphones as the driving force. Studies have shown that when children are not allowed used of computer devices, they learn better. What is it these wealthy tech executives know about their own products that their consumers don't? The answer, according to a growing body of evidence, is the addictive power of digital technology."[22] At the same time, the tech elite are happy to promote products that enslave the rest of us while lining their wallets.

"If research tells us that a tsunami of digital distractions is crashing into our lives, we need situational wisdom to answer three spiritual questions: Why are we lured to these distractions? What is a distraction in the first place? And perhaps the most foundational question of them all: What is the undistracted life?"[23]

For the tech-savvy Christian leader, whether pastor, musician, worship minister, sound engineer, or volunteer, the question must be asked: Do you own the tech, are you the master of the tech and instruments, or does the tech own and rule over you? Are you seduced by the power of tech? Have you fallen into the cultural perception that the power is the tech? What steps do you need to take to bring first your perception, then your use of technology, into total submission to the gospel?

Chapter 12

Survival

(in a Hyper-Connected World)

Humanity is acquiring all the right technology for all the wrong reasons. (R. Buckminster Fuller).

We are drowning in information while starving for wisdom (E.O. Wilson).

Enter at Your Own Risk

If you own a smart phone, you are hyper-connected in ways that should either frighten you or give you pause for concern. According to the *New York Times*, a massive database exists that tracks and records your every move. Your whereabouts, and most likely what you said when you were there, is tracked, recorded, sold, and archived. The information is used ostensibly for marketing research and niche advertising. But the implications go far beyond its stated use. Charlie Warzel and Stuart A. Thompson, New York Times recently reported: "In the months we've spent poring over this location data, speaking with people we were able to identify and reporting on the industry, one thing has become crystal clear: This is the decade we were brainwashed into surveilling ourselves."[1] In other words, by submitting to the conditions of use for the applications we use on our smart phones, we have given up the right to privacy.

The *New York Times* article goes on to say: "Think about it this way: Americans would be furious if the government required that every person must carry a tracking device that broadcast their location dozens of times each day, forever. And yet Americans have, with every terms of service agreement they click 'agree' on, consented to just such a system run by private companies. Tens of millions of Americans, including many children, are now carrying spies in their pockets. They go everywhere. To work, to the gym and then on their bedside tables. All in the service of better personalized alerts, turn-by-turn directions and more persuasive targeted advertising."

If you bank online, you are hyperconnected. AI algorithms have been developed in China that replace the loan officer.[2] It won't be long before we see use in the United States. The algorithm has the ability to analyze thousands of obscure facts about you and synthesize those facts into a profile that rates you as a consumer of loans. It analyzes the day of the week you applied, your height and weight, buying patterns, and financial history. Such algorithms are invasive to the point of knowing more about you than perhaps you know about yourself.

If you own a smart television set, watch YouTube videos, use the internet to shop for goods and services, you are hyperconnected. And so on.

Implied Consent

When we use technology, we are consenting legally to the use the designers intended for the technology to be used. Though the published intent is to provide better, more personalized services or cooler devices, it is in reality about maximizing the money we spend on goods and services and perhaps ultimately controlling how we live our lives. If this sounds sinister, there are those elements present.

The implications for the Body of Christ go far beyond simply being tracked or targeted for advertising. As mentioned in the previous chapter, artificial intelligence (AI) is being used in unprecedented manners. And those manners (e.g. applications) are already present during worship. Most carry smart phones or pads these days. Siri listens and Siri records what is said. But there is more. The console I use is run by a computer. It has the ability to recall any setting I have programmed into its memory—an extremely helpful tool. The next generation consoles will use AI to predict what the mix should be based on the environment. One could easily imagine AI interpreting the mix and determining the best mix for the instruments and musician skill level. Soon AI will be running the entire event, if we chose to let it. A number of manufacturers already have entire systems that require no operator whatsoever. There is no telling what an AI console will be able to do with the information it gathers and uses for worship. Will it analyze content not only for mix value but quality of information and perhaps bias? Will it report the information it gathers to a central database?

Some Christians have responded that they are not concerned because they have nothing to hide. The fact is that the amount of information gathered about you is unprecedented, exploitive, and compromises your freedom and liberty. The information may eventually be used to stop you from exercising your religious rights and freedoms.

It Was Very Good

Technology easily blinds us to the beauty that naturally surrounds us. We tend to want to improve on God's creation rather than seeing the sublime in all He has spoken. We want to fix what we believe is wrong both in our own bodies and in the world around us.

Genesis tells us that when God created (*ex nihilo*—out of nothing) all things, He said, and God saw everything that He had made, and behold, it was very good. (See Genesis 1:31).

Literally, the Hebrew says, "and behold, it was (abundantly) exceedingly good." No further embellishment was necessary, and no modification was required. We operate under a notion that we need to improve upon what God has made, but He says that it is exceedingly good in and of itself.

I am reminded of the altars the Children of Israel built to honor YAHWEH. When Israel crossed the Jordan, they walked on perfectly dry land. To commemorate, they constructed an altar for future generations to remember God's miraculous work. It is instructive to recall God's specific guidance in regard to how the altar was to be built. If you make me an altar of stone, *you shall not build it of hewn stones,* for *if you wield your tool on it you profane it* (Exodus 20:25 emphasis added).

The New Living Translation (NLT) uses the word "unfit" in place of profane.

> *If you use stones to build my altar, use only natural, uncut stones.* ***Do not shape the stones with a tool, for that would make the altar unfit for holy use.*** {emphasis added] (Exodus 20:25 NLT)

YAHWEH's altar was unfit and profaned if a tool was used to cut (modify) the stones used to build the altar. God says the stones that He made in creation are already exceedingly good and in no need of improvement or embellishment. The stones are as He intended, however they may appear.

When we make the assumption that we can improve on the Word of God, the creation of God, the very nature of God, we run the risk of profaning the very things God says are already exceedingly good. Creation cries out and begs for us to pay attention to its order and beauty (Romans 1). No technology can improve creation. No technology can bring a message clearer. Our voices, though they may at times sound imperfect to us, in and of themselves are a sweet aroma when lifted up in praise and worship of our heavenly Father. He is good. And His goodness is imputed to us. Nothing additional is required for our praise to be acceptable.

Involuntarily Unplugged

It was late summer. The music team, ministers, and staff arrived early to perform their weekly duties of setup and rehearsal. When we arrived, the power was out. It had been out for some time, and there was no credible information on when it would return. PG&E was performing blackouts in communities that were vulnerable to wildfires fueled by the strong Santa Ana winds. Our church sat in the fire line. Within minutes of realizing our condition, the team went to work moving the worship services to the playground, the backyard. The setup team rigged pavilions for shade. The sound team set up music stands and chairs for the musicians. The band practiced their song sets without amplification. The pastor was informed he would need to project his voice. Within less than an hour, everything was prepared and ready.

The worship services occurred on time and without a hitch. Since I was free from FOH responsibilities, I was able, to my delight, to focus solely on the words of the songs and on the message. The experience felt different. In this case, different was not a bad thing. At the end of the first service, the team gathered. The first comments were, in retrospect, surprising. "It worked" was said over and over. There was beauty in the simple sound of unmodified voices lifting praise and worship. Why would we marvel over that?

Since the experience, we have discussed the event and our reaction to it. We ponder the statement "it worked." Of course, it worked. Worship will happen with no power or sound reenforcement. Jesus spoke to thousands without a sound system or any technological assistance. Charles Spurgeon, the great 19th century preacher, preached to crowds of up to ten thousand people at one time with no sound system.[3]

We live in an evangelical culture that has adopted the axiom that worship services require technology. We seem bound to it with a fierce dependency. And as technology becomes more pervasive and invasive, will we know how to navigate it in a manner that does not compromise the gospel of Jesus Christ? With technology pushing its way into every nook and cranny of our lives, the question is raised: Can the Church survive in a technologically hyped-up world? The short answer—yes. It must and it will.

Too often, in our quest to win souls, we have turned to the world's tools to facilitate worship. If we believe we must use the tools of the world to attract the world, we are thinking about the gospel pragmatically and not spiritually. If we believe the power of the message is somehow contained in the stuff we use, we are denying the power of the resurrected Christ who "is before all things, and in him all things hold together." Jesus said that the Kingdom of God is built upon the rock of Peter's confession, "Jesus Christ is Lord." Christ is the unmovable cornerstone. As the Kingdom of God is built on that rock (Petra), the Kingdom moves and takes new territory in the lives and hearts of men. And "the gates of hell shall not prevail against it." To think, live, operate, and teach in the Kingdom means that we are dependent upon the cornerstone of Christ and Christ alone, not some fanciful means of winning souls, including technological tools. Souls are won and discipled in Christ by people, not machines. It's easy to lose sight of this.

Digital Distractions

We seem not to mind or concern ourselves with the implications of hyperconnectedness. Our culture thrives on a steady diet of distraction without consideration for the negative effects. All too often we pronounce that the good of being connected outweighs any bad.

"If research tells us that a tsunami of digital distractions is crashing into our lives, we need situational wisdom to answer three spiritual questions: Why are we lured to these distractions? What is a distraction in the first place? And perhaps the most foundational question of them all: What is the undistracted life?

Yes, we're all being digitally distracted to death (and we welcome it). And yes, all the studies say that we need less screen time (but we really don't want to hear that). As we humble ourselves and learn the art of digital self-control, we can speak into our generation with pointed insight into the purpose of our lives and what it means to flourish in the digital age—undistracted with eternal purpose in view."[4]

The question arises, "How do we manage our lives in a hyperconnected world?" From this author's perspective, it isn't easy. I depend on my computers to perform my consulting work and to write my manuscripts. I use Google search far too quickly to easily find a reference or even a biblical passage I cannot remember. I use internet data at times like I am drinking from a fire hose.

More Than Survival

To do more than survive, to overcome in an overly hyped technological world requires that we are first anchored in the truth of the Word and not in the worldly wisdom and trends around us. Rod Dreher recently lamented that the current popular form of worship, the *Celebrity Model,* using lights and smoke has already succumbed to the culture. Francis Chan describes this as Christians looking for external "life jackets" to keep them afloat instead of resting in the power of the Holy Spirit.[5] Chan also said, "Churches in the West often rely on external factors, like music, popular speakers, and light shows, to share the gospel instead of understanding that Jesus is enough."

Build Boundaries

The very ones who market their high-tech gadgets to us understand to some degree the correct relationship between technology and their children. When Steve Jobs was asked how his kids liked having iPhones and iPads, he replied that he would not let them have either. Jobs, like a number of Silicon Valley executives, subscribed to a form of education that does not depend on electronics and computers. These executives understand too well the downsides of being connected not only in terms of education but also in terms of privacy.

There are other factors as well. "Research has found that an eighth-grader's risk for depression jumps 27% when he or she frequently uses social media. Kids who use their phones for at least three hours a day are much more likely to be suicidal. And recent research has found the teen suicide rate in the US now eclipses the homicide rate, with smartphones as the driving force."[6]

Studies have shown that when children are not allowed the use of computer devices, they learn better. What is it these wealthy tech executives know about their own products that their consumers don't? The answer, according to a growing body of evidence, is the addictive power of "digital technology."[7] At the same time, the tech elite are happy to promote products that enslave the rest of us while lining their pocketbooks.

Give Rest

The principle of the rest is a theme that permeates the entire Bible, from Leviticus through the book of Hebrews. We enter rest from seeking approval from good works when we enter into a right relationship to Christ. We enter rest from all our works when we pass from this life into the next. Do we need to intentionally rest from our perception of what is pleasing to the world and enter into what is pleasing to God?

Some of the most meaningful moments in worship for me have been when the singing is *a cappella* or nearly so. Many years ago, while attending a leadership seminar at the Oracle Coliseum in Oakland, California, we were led in worship songs supported by 30,000 voices and no instruments. At the Promise Keepers rallies of the 1990s, thousands of men sang worship hymns and praises with the robustness that nearly drowned out the band. Sovereign Grace publishes CDs of hymns sung by pastors and ministers who attended the conference. Accompanied by either a piano or guitar, thousands of men's voices praise the Almighty. The sounds of praise in all of these are sweet sounds that fill and minister to the soul.

An antidote to the overly hyped, technology-driven worship service is to unplug from time to time and let the natural voices of the Kingdom of God on earth praise Him in all their human imperfection. When God chose to unplug our church service on the summer day when the power refused to turn on, we were humbly reminded of the natural sound born in every believer that must be heard. On that day, the voices of the congregation were clearly heard.

Unplugging can be as simple as singing choruses without the band or planning some songs to be solely *a cappella.* You may consider planning an entire service without technology. A planned "technology Sabbath rest" may be extended to other areas of life as well.

Technology Shabbat

Over the last number of years, the principle of Technology Shabbat has emerged. An early proponent of Technology Shabbat is Michael Medved. Michael is an American radio show host, author, political commentator, and film critic, who practices with his family a day of rest from technology.[8] Michael is a practicing Jew and celebrates the Sabbath, using the day to rest from technology. He calls it a kind of detoxing exercise. Michael's wife, Diane, writes: "By choosing one day regularly as an inviolate escape device, you liberate yourself from the tyranny of six other days' screen time." Diane speaks of a joyful experience that emerges by removing the influence of technology for periods of time.

Conclusion

In a hyperconnected world, we easily carry our attitudes about the world into our time of worship together. We turn authentic worship on its head when we depend on technology and the advances of technology in worship, rather than total dependence on Almighty God and Him alone. When we email, message, search Facebook and Twitter during the service, we are proclaiming our attitude. When those of us responsible for the worship service depend on technology (engaging sound, projection, lights, and smoke) rather than the power of the Almighty, we are proclaiming our attitude.

The power of the Holy Spirit alone is good and sufficient to accomplish His work. May we never forget that and pray that He reminds us. For those that may think otherwise, as I have expressly stately elsewhere in this book, I am not a Luddite. I am not one to hide or retreat completely from life in order to avoid technology. My life's work is based, rightly or wrongly, on the use of technology to improve communications and perform the heavy lifting of managing information. At the same time, it is incumbent on me and each believer in the all-sufficient work of Christ and His resurrection to place boundaries on the use and influence technology has on day-to-day living and as expressed in this book, within the time of worship that we share together.

Questions: Do you depend on technology—smart phone, internet, computers—to a degree that you cannot live without it? If you were to determine to take a rest from the use of technology for a day or a portion of the day, how would you accomplish it? How could you resist the temptation to violate your time of rest?

Team Discussion Questions: If you decided to do so, how would you lead your congregation to rest from technology in a worship service? What elements could you rest from and what elements would create a barrier to authentic worship if removed?

Food for Thought: Take the time to discuss or determine for yourself, is the music or the technology keeping you afloat or is it the power of Almighty God.

ENDNOTES

Introduction

[1] In most venues, the one FOH also performs the stage mix for the musicians.

[2] While "cult" is defined as worship, I am using the word to refer to a practice of the dishonoring type of worship.

[3] https://www.barna.com/research/state-church-2016/

[4] Orthopraxy follows orthodoxy (e.g. correct action or practice follows proper beliefs not the other way around.) Too often we seek the pragmatic—just go with what works. When we practice the pragmatic, we can easily contradict or negate theological beliefs because our actions are focused on results, rather than our beliefs informing our practice.

PART I

Chapter 1

[1] Sanctification is, over the life of the believer, the moment by moment process of God causing and directing us to be conformed to the image of Christ. See https://www.ligonier.org/blog/what-sanctification/

[2] Bob Kauflin, *True Worship—Seeking What Matters to God*, (Wheaton, Ill, Crossway, 2015), 20.

[3] 1 Corinthians 11:1— "Be imitators of me, as I am of Christ."

[4] Mark 10:45

[5] Rod Dreher, *The Benedict Option*, (New York, Sentinel, 2017), 132.

[6] In context see 1 Corinthians 9:19-23.

[7] More on authentic worship in PART II, Chapter 3.

[8] Thanks to my friend Brad Sousa for his insights into the generational issues. Brad has done a significant work in building strategies around the acknowledgement and accommodation of different age groups in the workforce. See https://www.forbes.com/sites/forbestechcouncil/2018/09/12/the-secret-to-accelerating-tech-adoption-from-multigenerational-perspectives/#4595307be7b3

[9] Dr. David Lee, *House of Worship: Business: Defusing Worship Wars*, Sound and Communications Magazine, April 2017, 19.

[10] Source: http://www.marketingteacher.com/the-six-living-generations-in-america/ There is disagreement among experts as to the exact breakdown of dates and groups. It should be noted that generational concepts are a very western notion. See https://www.thoughtco.com/names-of-generations-143547

[11] A pastor friend told me of a time he dismantled the worship band because he felt the congregation had become too dependent upon the band for worship. For a period of months, he and his wife lead singing using just an acoustic guitar. The break with the band allowed him time to rebuild the band and focus on the reasons for worship in the first place.
[12] Dr. Harold Best, *Unceasing Worship*, (Wheaton, InterVarsity Press, 2003), 77.
[13] Luke 12:34
[14] Charles R. Swindoll, *The Church Awakening: The Urgent Call for Renewa*l, (New York, FaithWords, 2010), 121.
[15] Matt Redman, *The Heart of Worship*, (Thankyou Music, copyright 1997)
[16] Swindoll, *The Church Awakening*, 139.
Chapter 2
[1] Romans 5:20 (KJV)
[2] Philippians 4:4

Part II Introduction

[1] Dictionary.com: https://www.dictionary.com/browse/stewardship?s=t
[2] John 14:15

Chapter 3

[1] Stephen Covey, *The 7 Habits of Highly Effective People*, (New York, Free Press, 2004), 95.
[2] Psalm 96:9
[3] Hebrews 12:28 – 29
[4] Horatio Spafford and Phillip Bliss, "It Is Well with My Soul," Gospel Songs No. 2, 1876
[5] Sing 2018 Video, https://gettymusicworshipconference.com/, accessed September 2018 [6] John Piper, *The Legacy of Sovereign Joy*, (Wheaton, Ill, Crossway Books, 2000), 40.
[6] John Piper, *The Legacy of Sovereign Joy*, (Wheaton, Ill, Crossway Books, 2000), 40.
[7] IBID,71.
[8] IBID, 40.
[9] David G. Peterson, *Engaging with God: A Biblical Theology of Worship*, (Wheaton, Illinois, InterVarsity Press, 2002), 98.
[10] I discuss the seduction of technology in the church in Chapter 12, "Who Will Stop the Train."
[11] C.S. Lewis, *Letters to Malcolm: Chiefly on Prayer*, (London: Geoffrey Bles, 1964), 4-5
[12] For excellent examples of various orders of service or liturgy's, see Mike Cosper's *Rhythms of Grace*.

[13] See Deuteronomy 32:46-47.
[14] Psalms 96, 98, and 149
[15] Best, *Unceasing Worship*, 146.
[16] https://hermeneutics.stackexchange.com/questions/19410/meaning-of-sing-to-the-Lord-a-new-song
[17] For an insightful discussion on a similar topic, "Would you wish your child to be dyslexic?", see *David and Goliath: Underdogs, Misfits, and the Art of Battling Giants* by Malcom Gladwell.
[18] C.S. Lewis, *Letters to Malcolm: Chiefly on Prayer*, 5.
[19] Authentic worship is the opposite of the popularized concept of Christian life being Moralistic Therapeutic Deism (MTD). MTD is described by: "1. 'A god exists who created and ordered the world and watches over human life on earth.' 2. 'God wants people to be good, nice, and fair to each other, as taught in the Bible and by most world religions.' 3. 'The central goal of life is to be happy and to feel good about one's self.' 4. 'God does not need to be particularly involved in one's life except when God is needed to resolve a problem.' 5. 'Good people go to heaven when they die.'" From Albert Mohler's blog: https://albertmohler.com/2005/04/11/moralistic-therapeutic-deism-the-new-american-religion-2/
[20] The amount of confusion and frustration this can cause is immeasurable. I only include the example because I am told by a pastor that he has seen it happen.
[21] The questions presented here are part of ongoing discussions I have had with Merril Smoak over several years. Merril is former Minister of Music at Trinity Church in Livermore, California.
[22] I applaud the challenging work of our worship leaders who consistently pick music in keys that can be sung by both females and males.

Chapter 4

[1] Bob Goff, *Everyone Always*, (New York, Nelson Books, 2018), 74.
[2] A favorite tongue-in-cheek saying of mine available on a T-Shirt that may be ordered online.
[3] Stephen Hawking and Leonard Mlodinow, *The Grand Design,* (New York, Bantam Books, 2010), 180.
[4] Richard Feynman, *The Value of Science,* 1955, 2. (http://www.faculty.umassd.edu/j.wang/feynman.pdf)
[5] Wenn, "O'Toole Wants Cleaners Note On His Tombstone," contactmusic.com, accessed July 2018, http://www.contactmusic.com/lawrence-of-arabia/news/otoole-wants-cleaners-note-on-his- tombstone_1018969
[6] Cinerama—an early wide-screen movie format that used three synchronized 35 mm projectors displayed side-by-side and edge blended to provide a very realistic experience (e.g., *How the West Was Won*)

[7] Exodus 35:10
[8] Exodus 39:43
[9] Dreher, *The Benedict Option*, 178.
[10] Francis Schaeffer, Jr., *Addicted to Mediocrity*, (Westchester, Crossway Books, 1981), 54.
[11] Dr. Harold Best, *Unceasing Worship*, (Wheaton, InterVarsity Press, 2003), 145-146.

Chapter 5

[1] Brad Sousa, a friend and colleague, provided the concept for this chapter during our conversations about the book. He suggested that tension is normal.
[2] Kliewer, Vernon, *Melody: Linear Aspects of Twentieth-Century Music*, (Englewood Cliffs, New Jersey: Prentice-Hall, 1975), 290.
[3] "Tension and Release in Music," Musical U Team, May 31, 2016, https://www.musical-u.com/learn/tension-in-music/
[4] Levi's real name is withheld by request.
[5] Paul is not saying that we are not to think highly of ourselves. Rather, not too highly. A good discussion question would be to ask what it means to not think too highly of one's self.

Chapter 6

[1] John Donne, *Meditation XVII, Devotions upon Emergent Occasions*, 1624.
[2] The philosophy behind the questions and the development of the questions were gathered over a series of interviews between Dennis and me.

PART III

Chapter 7

[1] See Ethan Winer's "Audio Myths Workshop," AES 2009. https://www.youtube.com/watch?v=BYTIN6wjcvQ
[2] Cyril M. Harris, *Handbook of Noise Control,* Volume 1 (New York, McGraw-Hill, 1957), 9.
[3] Mary C. Gruszka, "*TV Technology Newsletter*", February 23, 2018, https://www.tvtechnology.com/miscellaneous/the-importance-of-speech-intelligibility
[4] The challenges of planning worship overall for the six different generations alive today is addressed elsewhere in this book.
[5] I recently had an older member of the congregation ask me to turn down the music played between services because it hurt her hears. The level was lower than a typical conversation.

Chapter 8

[1] https://www.prosoundweb.com/channels/live-sound/quotable_quotes/

[2] If you are in the process of building a new space, it is best to consult your architect early in the process and insist that the space be designed not just aesthetically, but more importantly, acoustically.

[3] A reaction of solemnity and reverential silence should be part of every worship service no matter the style, the place, or the content of the message and music.

[4] The effects of temperature can manifest itself in a simple manner. (Ten degrees in temperature will change the speed of sound by 10 mph.) During rehearsal, I can dial in a desired sound for FOH, but when people arrive the sound is quite different. This is due to both the temperature of the room and the acoustics changing due to the presence of warm bodies.

[5] Shiny rocks may be gimmicks or glitzy equipment promoted for looks or impressive specifications alone.

[6] Those of you who know audio understand in this era, the specification would not be okay for an amplifier. But here, we are talking about a room (the acoustical space) and the electronics.

Chapter 9

[1] David Lee Wright, *Sound in the Gospel*, (NEBTHOS, 2016), 68.

[2] There are no guarantees in the marketplace but following these principles will lead you in the right direction.

[3] I used to work with a vendor who, if he did not know what I was talking about or didn't understand, would say "teach me." Saying "teach me" is a very humble phrase and is effective in meaningful dialog.

[4] https://www.prosoundweb.com/channels/live-sound/how-to-disappear-completely-my-year-of-working- without-corrective-eq/4/

Chapter 10

[1] Mixology = the art of developing the mix. The points made in this section are basic yet missing in overviews of FOH. For a more thorough look at mixology, see *Sound in the Gospel* by Magic Dave (listed in the Bibliography)

[2] See https://www.prosoundweb.com/channels/church/back-to-basics-despite-the-countless-tools- available-sometimes-simpler-is-better/2/

[3] Our lead vocalist calls me on stage regularly to make sure we agree on the monitor mix. Our perceptions of a correct mix differ at times. For a discussion on perception, refer to Chapter 7 introduction: *Perceiving Sound.*

[4] https://www.prosoundweb.com/channels/church/back-to-basics-despite-the-countless-tools-available-
sometimes-simpler-is-better/

[5] With apologies to Bill Hewlett and David Packard, founders of HP, who coined the acronym MBWA—Management by Walking Around

[6] dB is brief for decibel. Decibel is unit of measure for audio levels

[7] SPL = Sound Pressure Level. Measured with a Sound Level Meter and rated in dB. A normal conversation is 80 dB. A loud concert can be as high as 120 dB (which is defined as the threshold of pain).

PART IV

Chapter 11

[1] Source: https://en.wikipedia.org/wiki/Ken_Jennings

[2] https://en.wikipedia.org/wiki/Watson_(computer)

[3]https://www.ted.com/talks/ken_jennings_watson_jeopardy_and_me_the_obsolete_know_it_all?language=en

[4] For a fascinating look at how AlphaGo won GO, see the Netflix documentary, GO.

[5] For a comparision of how many lines of code are required from devices from smart phones to cars and even Google, see https://www.visualcapitalist.com/millions-lines-of-code/

[6] Notice how effortlessly we anthropomorphize computers!

[7] A number of "trans-portables" were introduced in the early 80s. Notably besides Osborne's were the IBM and Steven Kay's Kaypro.

[8] My father's view of ministry, not mine.

[9] I am not just technical. I serve other functions in the body including teaching and leading teams that teach the Bible.

[10] Novelist Daniel Silva uses a Number 2 pencil and Staples Yellow Legal pads to write his New York Times best-selling spy novels. David McCulloch writes all his award-winning biographies on a typewriter. Both believe the quality of their writing is directly affected by the tools they use.

[11] Thomas A. Stewart, *Intellectual Capital*, (New York, Doubleday, 1997), 7.

[12] https://en.wikipedia.org/wiki/The_medium_is_the_message

[13] https://scattergorieslists.com/top-9-negative-impacts-technology-society/

[14] The problem of finding all the factors of an exceptionally large number is one that quantum computers do well.

[15] https://thenextweb.com/artificial-intelligence/2018/02/06/heres-why-100-qubit-quantum-computers-
could-change-everything/

[16] "Deep learning is an artificial intelligence function that imitates the workings of the human brain in processing data and creating patterns for use in decision making. Deep learning is a subset of machine learning in artificial intelligence (AI) that has networks capable of learning unsupervised from data that is unstructured or unlabeled. Also known as deep neural learning or deep neural network." Source: https://www.investopedia.com/terms/d/deep-learning.asp

[17] https://www.technologyreview.com/s/604087/the-dark-secret-at-the-heart-of-ai/?utm
[18] https://www.cnbc.com/2017/02/27/smartphones-as-we-know-them-will-be-dead-in-five-years.html
[19] Legal scholar and ethicist Nita A. Farahany discussed the implications of the ability to decode and read your mood, emotional stability, and thoughts in short video at TED. See https://www.ted.com/talks/nita_farahany_when_technology_can_read_minds_how_will_we_protect_our_p rivacy?utm_source=newsletter_weekly_2018-12-01&utm_campaign=newsletter_weekly&utm_medium=email&utm_content=talk_of_the_week_image#t- 772620
[20] Exodus 20:8-11
[21] Paul calls us to be servants of Christ alone.
[22] Chris Weller, Business Insider, October 2017 discusses interviews with Bill Gates and Steve Jobs regarding how they parent with strict rules ragarding technology. The article is online at https://www.independent.co.uk/life-style/gadgets-and-tech/bill-gates-and-steve-jobs-raised-their-kids- techfree-and-it-shouldve-been-a-red-flag-a8017136.html
[23] Denzel Washington talks at length about smartphone addiction and the changes being made in our culture in an article found at https://www.desiringgod.org/articles/denzel-your-phone-is-changing-you

Chapter 12

[1] https://www.nytimes.com/2019/12/19/opinion/tracking-phone-data.html
[2] Kai-Fu Lee, AI Superpowers: China, Silicon Valley, and the New World Order, (Houghton Mifflin Harcourt, New York 2018), p. 112
[3] https://www.metropolitantabernacle.org/Church-Details/History
[4] https://www.desiringgod.org/articles/denzel-your-phone-is-changing-you
[5] https://www.gospelherald.com/articles/71877/20181030/francis-chan-satan-likes-isolate-christians-distract-iphones-keep-gospel.html
[6] https://www.independent.co.uk/life-style/gadgets-and-tech/bill-gates-and-steve-jobs-raised-their-kids-techfree-and-it-shouldve-been-a-red-flag-a8017136.html
[7] IBID
[8] http://www.michaelmedved.com/column/retreating-from-tech-one-special-day-every-week/

Bibliography

Theology References

Best, Dr. Harold, *Unceasing Worship,* Wheaton, InterVarsity Press, 2003

Chan, Francis, *Letters to the Church,* David C. Cook, 2018

Cosper, Mike, *Rhythms of Grace,* Wheaton, Crossway, 2013

Dreher, Rod, *The Benedict Option*, New York, Sentinel, 2017

Getty Music, Sing! Worship Conferences

Goff, Bob, *Love Does,* Nashville, Thomas Nelson, 2012

Kauflin, Bob, *True Worship – Seeking What Matters to God,* (Wheaton, Ill, Crossway, 2015)

Norsworthy, Grant, http://grantnorsworthy.com

Peterson, David G., *Engaging with God: A Biblical Theology of Worship,* Wheaton, Illinois, InterVarsity Press, 2002

Piper, John, *The Legacy of Sovereign Joy,* Wheaton, Ill, Crossway Books, 2000

Schaeffer, Francis, Jr., *Addicted to Mediocrity,* Westchester, Crossway Books, 1981

Swindoll, Charles R., *The Church Awakening: The Urgent Call for Renewal,* New York, FaithWords, 2010

Tomlin, Chris and Whitehead, Darren, *Holy Roar*, Nashville, Thomas Nelson, 2017

Sound System Design References

Davis, Don and Patronis, Eugene, Jr., *Sound System Engineering*, Burlington, Focal Press, 2006

Davis, Gary, *The Sound Reinforcement Handbook*, Yamaha Corporation of America and Gary Davis & Associates, 1990

Eiche, Jon F., edited by, *Guide to Sound Systems for Worship*, Yamaha Corporation of America, 1990

Harris, Cyril M., *Handbook of Noise Control, Volume 1*, New York, McGraw-Hill, 1957

Rossing, Thomas D., et. Al., *The Science of Sound*, 3rd Edition,

Sound and Communications Magazine, Testa Communications, New York

Synergistic Audio Concepts, an excellent professional worship on sound design. (http://www.prosoundtraining.com)

Winer's, Ethan, "*Audio Myths Workshop*," AES 2009 https://www.youtube.com/watch?v=BYTlN6wjcvQ

Wasem, James, *Great Church Sound, A Guide for the Volunteer*, Missoula, Montana, Great Sound Institute, 2015

Vear, Tim, *Audio Systems Guide, Houses of Worship*, published by Shure Audio Institute, 2015

Wright, David Lee ("Magic Dave"), *Sound in the Gospel*, NEBTHOS, 2016

Resource on church acoustics: http://www.jdbsound.com/work/b1.html

Other Resources

Covey, Stephen, *The 7 Habits of Highly Effective People*, New York, Free Press, 2004

Feynman, Richard, *The Value of Science*, 1955 (http://www.faculty.umassd.edu/j.wang/feynman.pdf)

Gladwell, Malcom, *David and Goliath: Underdogs, Misfits, and the Art of Battling Giants*, New York, Little, Brown and Company, 2013

Hawking, Stephen and Mlodinow, Leonard, *The Grand Design*, New York, Bantam Books, 2010

Stewart, Thomas A., *Intellectual Capital*, New York, Doubleday, 1997

Acknowledgements

First and foremost, I am grateful to my Lord Jesus Christ who has called me to his kingdom and to the eternal salvation that cannot be shaken or revoked. It is His work alone that makes our labors and service not only meaningful, but effective in the Kingdom of God.

I am deeply grateful to Karen, my wife of almost 50 years. She has loved me unconditionally from the moment she met me and brings an uncanny wisdom and a gift of discernment to our lives. She sees things as they truly are, not as I hope they would be. She is my abiding best friend, my counselor, and a constant source of smiles, laughter, and fun. I am also grateful for my daughters, Heather and Holly and my son-in-law Roy. They are a source of incredible joy – as is the case with all our grandchildren – and an enduring source of wisdom. I enjoy the family thoroughly and gather great strength and encouragement from them in these troubling times.

To my brother Dennis Dirks, a genuine servant-leader, a deep and heartfelt thank you. Dennis is my brother, best friend, and mentor. His insights and encouragement honed carefully from a lifetime of ministry as pastor, professor, and seminary leader has helped shape the ideas presented here.

A thank you to Dan Barnett, Timothy Berg, Pastor Andy Cochran, Bob Fischer, Joe Pacheco, Pastor Corwin Wong, and Brad Sousa for their review of the manuscript and thoughtful insights and suggestions. Each has been an encouragement to me in the process of writing and working through the details.

And last but not least to Merril Smoak, my life-long friend, coworker in the faith, and music minister. It was through Merril that I learned that the relationship between music minister/leader and FOH/engineer can be productive, engaging, and a grand service in the Kingdom. When Merril invited me to guest lecture in his MDIV class at Gateway Seminary, the seed for this book was planted. Thank you Merril!

About the Author

David lives in Livermore, California. He is a consultant in Information Technology and currently leads the sound/media team at Brentwood Bible Fellowship, Brentwood, CA. David is a former Distinguished Member of Technical Staff at Sandia National Laboratories. He has worked as sound system designer and FOH his entire career. David also teaches Bible classes and is guest lecturer on the topic The Sounds of Worship at Gateway Seminary, San Francisco Bay Area. David is married to Karen, his wife of nearly 50 years. He has two daughters, Heather and Holly, son-in-law Roy, and 5 grandchildren, Emma, Helen, Jack, Will and Levi.

Made in the USA
Las Vegas, NV
16 December 2021